It Only Happens Now and Then …

A personal memoir by

Mary Patricia Hamilton

Published by Hamilton House
Lakewood, NJ
fitzihamilton@yahoo.com

Library of Congress Control Number: 2011907501
ISBN: 978-0-615-48679-6

For my grandchildren:

Seamus Fitzgerald

Patricia Kim

Mary Patrice

Stephen Carey

James Noel

Declan Diego

Peter Lee

Margaret Mary

Claire Noel

Meaghan Fitzgerald

Julia Ellen

Bridgett Fitzgerald

Francis Xavier

Maura Grace

Aleth Ellen

Laurel Mary

Sean Brewer

I would like to especially thank my eldest granddaughter, Patty Kim, who was always asking me to tell her stories about what it was like when I was young and who inspired me to write the stories down.

Today I have been as it were a child again. In telling you my life, I seemed to live it all over again. And I saw and felt it all just as when it was really happening. There are so many things we never think of until one day the memory awakens. And now you have heard the story of an old woman's life from its first beginning right up to this very day. And I could not help weeping for joy to think I had been so happy ...

Orulo, an Inuit woman, as quoted by Knud Rasmussen in *Across Arctic America*

Contents

Photographs

Prologue

I have been thinking of "telling my story" for a while now, and after speaking recently to my son Phillip who told me he was going to write a book, but was waiting until I died, I have decided, on the advice of a dear friend, to write it down before I "go to the great beyond" so that you will hear my side of the story.

As I sit here, I wonder how far back I should go. I guess I'll go all the way back to Ireland where it all began. My mother, Nellie Carey, and father, Joe Fitzgerald, were both born in Waterford, Ireland, and they lived all their young years very close to one another. My mother, born on March 31st, 1901, was the twelfth child of the thirteen children in her family[1]. She told me that her older brothers (there were eight of them) were all in Ireland during the time of the famous Irish Rebellion, and she thinks they were in the old IRA. She said she could remember during that time, around 1913, when she was about twelve years old, all her brothers' bicycles had to be disassembled every evening and hung in the barn. This was a British rule so that no one had access to the roads in the dark. One night British troops came to their cottage looking for her brothers. They found that one of the bicycles was missing and so they beat her brothers who were at home. She had a vivid recollection of that night, but she never mentioned any other specific events related to the struggle for Irish independence. Waterford in the south-east of Ireland was never the scene of much conflict.

---

[1] We always celebrated my mother's birthday on March 31st, but the official birth report filed in the summer of 1901 lists her birthday as April 30th.

My father, born August 8th, 1899, had no recollection of problems with the British. My mother used to joke and say that was because the "Fitz's," as she called them, were British sympathizers. People who owned their own property at that time in Ireland were considered to be pro-British. And the fact that my father played cricket, an English game, and not hurling and Irish football like her brothers was another clue.

In any event, my mother told me one day that she went out with my father since she was a very young woman. He was the only beau she ever had in Ireland. She said my Dad was a most handsome fellow, a beautiful dancer and considered to be a "great catch" since he was the oldest son of Tom Fitzgerald of Knockhouse. Knockhouse was, and still is, a very large farm in Waterford (over 250 acres) and eventually, my Dad would inherit this, as he was the oldest son of the Fitzgerald family. In Irish families, the property was always left to the oldest son. My mother said that my Dad was a very hard worker and practically ran the farm. Being the oldest son, he had a great deal to do with the rearing of the younger children of whom there were eight sisters and seven brothers.

Even though my Dad worked very hard on the farm, he always went dancing on weekends. These dances were held in a field at the end of the Knockhouse property. All the brothers would erect a wooden dance floor on Saturday, and people would come from miles around to attend these country dances. They were at a "crossroad" where two roads met at the end of the field. Thus they were called "crossroads" ceili dances.

Wonderful dancing went on here, as all the country people were marvelous dancers. In those days, the only entertainment for young people was dancing. My mother was a beautiful dancer and so was Joe Fitzgerald. It was at these dances that they started their courtship. My mother had beautiful long red hair, and my Dad used to tell me that was how she "captured" him … that long red hair.

They had been going out for a while, when my mother realized that there was no way Joe Fitzgerald's father, my grandfather Thomas Fitzgerald, was going to agree to this match as he had it in his head that his oldest son would marry a farmer's daughter and combine the farms. He even had the girl picked out. Her name was Josie McGraw; she was an only child, and her father's land abutted my grandfather's land. He considered her a "perfect match." That was the way matches were made in Ireland in the old times. It was a way of increasing one's property.

Knowing this was the way it was going to be, Nellie Carey, who was trained as a dressmaker, went to the United States where she had an older brother. She sailed on the R.M.S Adriatic and arrived in New York on June 6th, 1925. Ellis Island was not used for emigration processing after 1924 so she by-passed that famous way station and landed directly in Manhattan. After some years in the U.S., she returned to see her parents, and when she was riding her bike into town, along came Joe Fitzgerald. He told me that as soon as he saw her "gorgeous red hair, that was it," and he decided then and there to marry her.

He went to his father, told him what he was going to do, asked him about building a house at the bottom of the lane on their property for him and Nellie Carey, and his father refused and said he would have to wait until he

inherited Knockhouse. Of course, Nellie Carey said she
wouldn't wait as she had seen too many girls "waiting"
and too many girls "left waiting" when the inheritance of
the farm came. So off she went again to the United
States. Shortly after that, Joe Fitzgerald asked his father
for whatever was due him in the way of wages as he had
worked diligently on the farm without ever getting true
wages. His father always gave him spending money when
he went to town, as he was his oldest son, and he did not
want it to appear that he didn't have money. But he was
never paid for all his labor. His payment was going to
come when he got the farm. When he told his father that
he was going to America to marry Nellie Carey, he said his
father was very generous and he traveled to the United
States very comfortably. He sailed from Queenstown on
November 9th, 1929 on the R.M.S. Samaria and he arrived
in New York ten days later on November 19th. His
brothers and sisters could not believe that their father
would let him go, but my grandfather was a stubborn man
according to all the stories that I have heard.

My Dad's life in America began just as the Great
Depression was getting under way, but it never seemed to
affect him. His years on the farm had taught him how to
work and he was very good with people. In New York,
he always had a job and he always maintained a great,
faith-based optimism.

In 1931, Joe Fitzgerald married Nellie Carey on
Thanksgiving Day in Saint Francis of Assisi Catholic
Church in Brooklyn. The reason they were married on
Thanksgiving was because it was a holiday, and since they
were Irish and new in the country, they weren't into
American customs like Thanksgiving. Besides it was a day

off from work. So instead of having a big Thanksgiving dinner, they had a wedding reception.

My Dad's first job was in Gristede's, a food chain in New York City where they hired "good looking Irishmen who knew how to wear a bow tie." At least, that is the story my Dad told me. My Dad was a very natty dresser and loved to get dressed up. As a matter of fact, I don't believe I ever saw my Dad disheveled. He was always a gentleman.

After that position, he took a job in the Hotel Belvedere on 48th Street in the heart of New York City. He started out, I believe, as an elevator operator and became the Superintendent of Service. I remember a few stories from the early days of their marriage. My mother told me that she would meet my father at 48th Street and 8th Avenue, where he worked, and the two of them would walk home all the way to Brooklyn. It was quite a long way from 48th street in Manhattan all the way down to the tip of the island, and then across the Brooklyn Bridge and several more miles before they got home. My mother said it was quite a jaunt, but they didn't mind. They walked all the time in Ireland. The two of them actually walked through the Lincoln Tunnel the day it was opened, and they were at the front of the crowd leaving New York City, but when they got to the other side in New Jersey, they were made to turn back because the people in charge of the opening day festivities at the Tunnel wanted to allow the dignitaries, namely Grover Whelan, the official greeter of New York, out of the tunnel first. That was an amazing story, and I can't imagine how scary it was to walk through the tunnel thinking that you were finally coming to the end on the New Jersey side of the Hudson River, only to be told to turn back and return to the New York side.

My mother worked for a short time after her marriage, but she was happy to leave her dressmaking job and become a homemaker. As a dressmaker, my mother worked for a man who made evening gowns for rich women. The gowns were very intricate with lots of beading and sequins. Most of the clientele who frequented this dressmaking establishment were rich and heavy-set women. My mother hated to make an evening gown in a size 18. She thought evening gowns should be worn only by women with beautiful figures. It was almost as if she were an artist and hated to see her creation displayed on a rich matronly body. What used to drive her crazy was the fact that these fat women were not happy when they put the gowns on, because they thought they should look like Carole Lombard when in fact they looked like Marie Dressler (that was my mother's opinion). She said they were impossible to please as it was not possible to make a size 18 woman look like a size 8 girl. So she was glad to leave dressmaking behind her. As an aside, she did make the comment to me that the greatest invention with regard to sewing was the zipper. Before the zipper, all the dresses were closed with "hooks and eyes," and it took hours to sew these into the dresses.

My parents had three children, Thomas William Fitzgerald, named after his two grandfathers, naturally; Mary Patricia Fitzgerald, named after my two grandmothers, and Joseph Patrick Fitzgerald, named after my Dad. My Dad was into tradition and doing things the way they had been done for years such as the naming of one's children after grandparents, etc.

So that was the beginning of my family.

Now for my story, or my "memoir" as my grandchildren call it, told here in my own voice for the memory of those whom I have loved.

My parents, Nellie Carey and Joseph Fitzgerald, on their wedding day in 1931

It Only Happens Now and Then ...

Brooklyn

I was born on March 3rd, 1935 in Peck Memorial Hospital. My mother and father were Irish immigrants, and I was their second child. I have an older brother, Tom, and a younger brother, Joseph. We had, as I recall, a rather ordinary childhood. We lived on Bedford Avenue in an apartment house, on the 3rd floor. This was very important because we were at the top of Brooklyn, near Eastern Parkway, and my mother said that with cross ventilation, you could always get a great breeze on the 3rd floor and up. This was necessary because in the summers, it was stifling hot in Brooklyn (at times it would be over 100 degrees) and to Irish people the heat was unbearable. Of course, in the winter, the 3rd floor was freezing because the heat had a hard time coming up in these old apartments. In the cold winter mornings, my mother would put all our clothes on the radiator to heat them up. While we were getting dressed, she made us breakfast consisting of a bowl of oatmeal and an egg, usually soft boiled. We had egg cups and the egg was put in the cup, the top cut off, plenty of salt was sprinkled on the egg, and the bread was toasted, buttered and cut in small slices so we could dip it into the egg. My mother called these concoctions "googie eggs" and I loved them. This is the type of breakfast my mother had in Ireland and she felt it prepared us for the long walk to school on a cold winter's day. As I recall, this was the breakfast for the whole school year. Another part of our daily breakfast was a teaspoon of cod liver oil. It was awful and we hated it, but I think it kept us healthy.

On Sundays, my Dad cooked breakfast, and he made the most delicious bacon and eggs. My brothers and I went to the nine o'clock Mass without eating breakfast because in those days, one did not eat before going to Communion, and so when we returned from Mass, my Dad had breakfast ready. We usually had wonderful rolls on Sunday. They came from the Jewish bakery on Rogers Avenue, and they were delicious. I believe that my mother went to early Mass in order to get us ready for church and my Dad went to a later Mass, as he was an usher at church.

Sundays were family days in Brooklyn, and they were spent going to church, then having lunch, then going for a family outing either to Prospect Park or to Sheepshead Bay, and then home for Sunday dinner. Usually, my mother did not go on these outings, as she was home getting the "Sunday Dinner" ready. Sunday dinner was a very special time in our house and the houses of all our friends. Since we were all Irish Catholics, going to Mass was of primary importance, and after that was the "Sunday Dinner." Almost every Irish family observed the custom of eating a great dinner on Sunday. The bill of fare for this dinner consisted of a roast of some kind: beef, lamb, ham or chicken, with plenty of mashed potatoes, vegetables and gravy. Relatives would be traveling from the Bronx to Brooklyn and vice versa. It was a time for visiting and talking about old times in Ireland and about family at "home." Of course, "home" to my Mom and Dad, and their friends, was Ireland. Irish music was played in our house and people would sing great old songs. Sunday was a day on which no one worked ... except, of course, the women who prepared the meal. In looking back, I think these women were wonderful. They took great care of their families and gave them the security that comes from having a clean house and good food and visiting friends and relatives who had great wit and personality. Most of these Sunday visits were arranged with relatives in the Bronx and Manhattan and Queens without the benefit of the telephone. None of our family friends or relatives had a telephone in those days, and I often wonder how they made these arrangements and arrived with children in tow for Sunday dinner. But somehow they did. I guess most of the details were worked out by mail. In those days, I remember seeing postcards coming and going. I remember that we had "penny postcards." One could buy a postcard in the post office or the drug store for a penny and dash off a message. I also remember that the mail was delivered twice a day, and that on every corner in Brooklyn there was a mailbox. Mail was the major method of communication.

As we grew older, my Dad changed the Sunday dinner hour from four in the afternoon to 1 o'clock because it allowed us children to go out socializing. He would accept no excuse for missing Sunday dinner. You had to be there at 1 o'clock or else you would be in great trouble. My Dad was a gentleman and rarely ever raised his voice, but we knew when he was serious, and serious he was about Sunday dinner.

After dinner, we were allowed to go wherever we wanted to go, but we always had to be home by dark. We were so fortunate that we lived in a neighborhood where there was public transportation to any place we wanted to go; and when we were small, the subway was five cents, and a five cent ride (including transfers) would take us to Manhattan or Queens or the Bronx.

From our apartment on Bedford Avenue, we could walk to the Brooklyn Botanical Garden which was wonderful.

I particularly loved the Japanese Garden. It was like stepping into another world. Right next to the Botanical Garden was the Brooklyn Museum, which was full of wonderful things to see. I can remember going there on a Saturday afternoon with my best friend, Betty Keane. Our favorite exhibit was the one in which they had a fully furnished Federalist home. Since Betty and I both lived in apartments and had never been in an actual house, this was like visiting a beautiful colonial home furnished with the loveliest couches, tables, rugs, silver and china. The dining room table in this exhibition was always set for dinner, and I remember being most impressed with that. To this day, I attribute my fascination with a well-set table to my adventures in the Brooklyn Museum.

After wandering through the museum, we could continue on to the Brooklyn Public Library on Grand Army Plaza, and then a short distance away from the museum was Prospect Park, a world class public park. A big part of our Sunday journeys was walking to all these places or maybe roller-skating which was great fun.

My parents were into walking and miles and miles meant nothing to them, as they were raised in Ireland where walking was the primary mode of transportation. Bicycling was also big in Ireland, but in Brooklyn, living in an apartment, there was no way to have a bicycle. We did learn to ride a bicycle, however, as my parents believed this was important. So on the Sundays when we didn't go to the museum, park, etc., we went to Sheepshead Bay on the trolley. It was five cents and it was like taking an amusement ride through Brooklyn to reach the water of Sheepshead Bay. Many people were strolling along the water, and at the end of the stroll, there was a bicycle store that rented bicycles for 25 cents an hour. It was a great treat for us to rent bikes, and my Dad would run along with us and teach us how to do it. It didn't take more than an hour to learn to ride the way my Dad was teaching us. After we could ride, my brothers and I would go along the bicycle path, and my Mom and Dad would just sit and watch the boats go by. Before we took the trolley home, my Dad would stop at Lundy's Restaurant where they had counter service outside by large windows, and he could sit there and have a beer and a plate of clams. My brothers and I would go with him and he would let us eat the oysterettes, which were small salty crackers. To us, this was a great treat.

Another favorite outing of my father's was a trip to Donegal Hill in Prospect Park. On Sundays, this particular section of the park was a gathering place for picnicking Irish immigrants. There was a big field where some of the men played Irish football. Although my father did not play this game, he and my mother were fans of the sport, and it gave them a chance to socialize with other Irish people. My brothers and I would play with the other little Irish kids while our parents talked about the "old country." My father usually brought his portable radio to the park on these Sundays because he liked to lie down on the grass and listen to the Dodgers baseball game while he was watching the Irish football.

Some Sundays, when it rained, we would be invited for "coffee and cake" at the apartment of Norwegian friends of ours who lived across the street. These people were "The Jacobsons," and they had this wonderful ritual of serving coffee and cake at four o'clock on Sunday afternoons in the living room on the coffee table. I remember it was the first time I had ever seen the coffee table used for that purpose. We had a coffee table, but we ate all our food in the dining room. I thought it was elegant. Mrs. Jacobson had a silver coffee pot, something she had brought with her from Europe. The dessert was always homemade. Usually it was waffles dusted with powdered sugar that Mrs. Jacobson would make earlier in the week and store in a tin box. They were so delicious. I always wanted to be able to make them, but I never found the recipe. While we were visiting at this apartment on Sunday, we listened to the radio, and at five o'clock everyone stopped talking and we listened raptly to "The Shadow Knows" and the adventures of Lamont Cranston and his friend, Margo Lane. It was a scary, spooky show, but we let our imaginations go wild, and we were enthralled by the mystery of it.

We lived at 1585 Bedford Avenue. An interesting mix of people lived in the building. The superintendent was an Italian, Mr. Tessei. He was a great super, as I recall, and he kept the building spotless. He seemed to me to be always shining the brass mailboxes. There were a lot of Jewish families, and they seemed to be always cooking gefilte fish, or at least that's what my mother said. And then there were a couple of Irish families. We all got along; it was like the League of Nations.

I do remember that my Grandmother Fitzgerald came from Ireland to see us in 1939, the summer before the war, and she stayed only a short while because of the increasingly ominous news about the oncoming conflict. She wanted to return to Ireland before she got stuck in America and couldn't leave. It was a very dangerous time to travel, as it was thought Germany might attack passenger ships on the Atlantic at any time. My Grandmother would have well remembered the infamous sinking of the Lusitania by a German U-boat off the coast of Ireland in 1915 during World War I. In that attack over a thousand passengers and crew perished.

When my Grandmother returned to Ireland, there was a serious shortage of tea and sugar, and every couple of weeks my mother and I would walk to the post office and mail a bundle to Ireland. In it would be clothes for the children, as everything was in short supply, and also without fail, a bag of loose tea and two pounds of sugar, as the Irish had great difficulty drinking tea without sugar.

It Only Happens Now and Then …

Uncle Chris

I couldn't write my memoir without a chapter about my Uncle Chris, who came to live with us for a while after leaving the Brothers of Charity. He had been sent to Belgium at the age of twelve to join this religious order and be educated, and had not seen my father, his brother, in over twenty years. When he was eventually assigned to Boston, he got in touch with my Dad, and they renewed their long lost relationship.

Chris told my Dad that he was not suited to this calling and asked him if he could help him get himself out of his situation. My Dad did everything he could for him, and when he was released from the order, he came to live with us.

He was the most charming and handsome Irishman one could ever hope to meet, and now he was an eligible bachelor, and my mother was all the time trying to fix him up with the many single Irish girls that she and my Dad knew, but it seemed no one was right for him.

And then one night he went to a dance in Manhattan at a place called the Tuxedo Ballroom. The ballroom was located on 86th Street in Manhattan and it was the meeting place of Irish greenhorns. An Irish greenhorn was someone who had just come to the United States from Ireland and wanted to socialize with other Irish young people. You could always tell who the "greenhorns" were at the Tuxedo Ballroom because they wore their ties outside their sweaters. For the record, Uncle Chris is not a man who wore his tie outside his sweater. It was at the Tuxedo Ballroom one fateful night that Uncle Chris met Margaret Larkin who would become our beloved Aunt

Peggy. As he told us the story, Margaret was the "most beautiful" girl he had ever seen and he was going to marry her. Needless to say, my mother was delighted because she was going to lose her star boarder. So everyone in the family encouraged the romance. He was supposed to meet Margaret the next week at the same dance, but she never showed up as she had promised. He was beside himself, and it was difficult living with him. Saturday after Saturday, for six weeks, he showed up at the dance hoping to see Margaret, but she never arrived. Finally, on the seventh Saturday, there she was. He went over to her and asked her where she was for the six weeks, and she told him the priest in the rectory where she worked had died, and the whole church had been in a period of mourning for all these weeks. My uncle was so happy to see her that he vowed never to be separated from her again. He proposed on the spot and she accepted him. She said she knew the first time she met him that she was going to marry him. He sailed home that evening and announced he was getting married, and we were all wildly enthusiastic about the prospect of meeting this girl he kept raving about.

Finally, the big day came and he was bringing Margaret for Sunday dinner. When an Irishman brings someone home for Sunday dinner, it is a very special day. My mother was so glad Chris was getting married and so anxious that Margaret would like his family that she went out and bought a new oriental rug for our dining room. She spent days polishing and cleaning the apartment so that Margaret would never think of not marrying Chris. I remember that she sent me downstairs to sit on the stoop and watch for them coming from the subway. When I saw them, I was to ring the bell to let her know they were approaching. The first time I saw my Aunt Peggy, as we came to call her, I remember thinking, "She looks just like Gene Tierney, the movie actress." They were the most handsome couple. Both of them had jet black hair and wonderful smiles, and their dispositions were so charming. Needless to say, we were all enchanted with Peggy and they married and stayed married happily for more than 50 years. They had a tremendous influence on my life and the life of everyone who came in contact with them. They were a true model of Christian marriage.

Uncle Chris and Aunt Peggy at their wedding

It Only Happens Now and Then ...

Crossing the Atlantic

Continuing with my memoir, my life was very simple, although I must say that most children did not travel on a vacation, on an ocean liner, across the Atlantic when they were two years old. But in 1937, my mother took me and my brother Tom to Ireland to meet our grandparents. I have very little recollection of this, but my brother, Tom, can remember being in Ireland. He was 4 1/2 at the time. He remembers being on a big ship, the Georgic, and then walking down a gangplank to a smaller boat in Queenstown, Ireland. He particularly remembers the baggage being lowered from the big ship onto the smaller boat which was called a tender. The small boat was necessary because the port in Ireland was too small to allow a large liner to dock. My mother told me the ocean voyage was horrendous, and she was seasick for the whole trip and never left her cabin. She had no idea who was taking care of us, as she was too sick to care. Can you imagine two little kids on this type of voyage without their mother to care for them? I guess someone was watching out for us because we survived to tell the tale. I was supposedly a great talker, even at two, because my mother told me that when we were staying with our grandparents and after she went out for the evening, her father, my grandfather, would get me out of bed, tie me into a chair near the fire and talk to me. My mother would return home and find me asleep in the chair next to my grandfather. She said he thought I had such an interesting way of talking. It must be that he liked my accent which was very different from an Irish child. My grandfather had a pony and trap (a little two wheel cart) and he was always taking my brother and me for rides around the roads. At that time, 1937, there were very few cars in Ireland. Everyone travelled on bicycles. As a matter of fact, once when my mother was riding with my brother on the back of her bicycle, he caught his heel in the spokes of the wheel and had to be rushed to the infirmary for stitches.

Passport photo of Tom and me 1937

My grandfather with his trap and pony

It Only Happens Now and Then …

My grandfather in his work clothes circa 1900

It Only Happens Now and Then ...

The War Years

Most of my childhood was spent during wartime. It is strange that neither I, nor my brothers can remember much of World War II. All I can remember is saving gum wrappers, any kind of silver paper, grease, newspapers, all for the war effort which I mostly heard about when I went to school. No one in our building had a telephone, and few had a radio. We did have a radio, but children didn't listen to the radio during the school year because they had to do their homework, and if we did listen, it was to the Lone Ranger if all our homework was done. How we loved the Lone Ranger. Whenever it was going to be on, even my brother, Tom, did his homework.

My brothers and I went to St. Francis of Assisi School in Brooklyn. We lived in St. Ignatius parish, but because our parish didn't have a school of its own, we went to school in the next parish which was St. Francis of Assisi. When I first went to St. Francis, I was five years old, and I was enrolled in the kindergarten which was taught by an elderly woman. As I remember, my mother went with me the first day, and she took my little brother, Joe, along in his carriage. When we got there my mother told the teacher, I believe her name was Miss Laughlin, that even though my name was Mary Patricia Fitzgerald, she would prefer it if they would call me "Patsy" as that is what I had always been called since birth. In no uncertain terms, Miss Laughlin told my mother that I was to be called Mary because that was my name. That was news to me, as I always thought my name was "Patsy." So Miss Laughlin kept referring to me as "Mary," and I had no idea who she was talking to, as I thought I was Patsy and not Mary. Finally, she explained to me that my real name was Mary Patricia and that my parents, for some strange reason, just called me "Patsy." It probably was a very traumatic experience for me, but I got over it.

My brother, Tom, tells me it was about three quarters of a mile walk to school, downhill going and uphill returning, and we walked it every day, rain or shine. I remember that my mother would not give me or my brothers the three cents for the trolley, as she said walking was good for us, and that she had walked much farther to school in Ireland. So that was the end of the argument.

Everyday my brother Tom and I walked down Rogers Avenue where we met up with Betty and Mary Keane who would become lifelong friends of our family. Tom and Mary talked and Betty and I trailed behind them. We returned from school the same way, and I can remember I always wore braids, and every afternoon one of my braids would be out of the ribbon. My brother always complained to my mother that I was so sloppy he didn't want to walk with me. I said we should cut my hair short, like Betty's, but my Dad would not hear of it. He said a woman's hair was her crowning glory, and my hair was not to be cut, and that was "an order." In our house, my mother's favorite expression when she wanted us to do anything was "Your father left strict orders!" When we heard her say that, we knew it was serious.

By today's standards, St. Francis of Assisi School was not politically correct. All the smart kids sat on one side of the class and all the "dumb" kids sat on the other side of the class. You were seated in the row depending on your average on your report card. That is, the smartest child sat in the first row, first seat, and on and on until you got to the last row, last seat, whereupon sat the stupidest (or thought to be the stupidest) child in the class. Many times, but not all times, I found myself with the great honor of being in the first row, first seat.

Jim, my future husband, found himself early in his career in the last row, last seat. Of course, he was there because he couldn't see the blackboard due to bad vision, and he was thought to be stupid. By the time he was in the 3rd grade, he had glasses and began to move up in the seating arrangement and was in the 3rd row when he graduated. There were six rows in the class, and if you made it over to the 3rd row, you were beginning to look "smart." The whole system was kind of crazy, but it worked, as some of the children loved the competition of trying to get into that first row. The teachers in our school were not into worrying about the "feelings" of their students; rather they worried about educating them to be able to make a living in a competitive society. And they were very successful at that. In those days, schools were a very competitive experience, and it was the fun of achieving that spurred on most of the children.

It was like a game to us to see who would have the highest grades, and this competitive spirit was heartedly encouraged by the nuns and priests. As a matter of fact, the midterm and final grades of the students in our parish were published in the Sunday bulletin for the whole parish to see. My mother was particularly keen that we showed up in the bulletin with high grades. She was never satisfied with the grade. For instance, if we had a 95% average, she would want to know why it wasn't 96%. She would not tolerate any grade below a 90%, and if we didn't achieve it, we were rewarded with a "whack" on the head. My brothers and I knew what was coming if we didn't get a 90%, and Joseph and I never got below a 90, but once in a while my brother Tom would get below 90, and my mother was not happy with this.

Discipline was very strict in St. Francis, and getting hit with a ruler was an everyday occurrence if you didn't behave. Of course, this happened mostly to the boys. In the 5th grade, the boys and girls went to separate buildings and Holy Cross Brothers taught the boys and the Sisters of Saint Joseph continued to teach the girls.

We had a wonderful education in this school. I am very thankful to the nuns who taught us how to read and how to write with the Palmer Method. We spent hours drawing circles, diagonal lines, etc. so that we would get the rhythm of a penmanship that flowed. Today, this activity would probably be called "developing hand/eye coordination." The nuns placed a great emphasis on penmanship and we were graded in this subject. It was a big part of our education. I think they were very successful with the girls, but I can't say the same for the boys. When I get a letter from an acquaintance today, I can always tell if she was educated by the nuns. I can truly say that all the girls who graduated from St. Francis had a beautiful handwriting.

When I reminisce about the education at St. Francis, I am amazed at how proficient these nuns were at getting immigrant children ready to assimilate into society. Every Wednesday afternoon, they had some cultural event going on in the auditorium. It might be an Irish Tenor singing beautiful ballads or an Italian baritone singing opera. All the people who performed were members of the parish who had been prevailed upon by the nuns to give a performance for the children. And if there was no one to perform, we would take out our music books and sing songs: patriotic songs, Stephen Foster songs, etc.

Family outing during the war

Celebrating my First Communion with Joe and Tom 1943

It Only Happens Now and Then ...

Occasionally, they would run a movie for us on this huge projector that made all sorts of noise. Where they got the movie projector, I will never know, and who ran it, I don't know either. It was probably a fireman or someone like that. Firemen were always called upon to help out as they worked strange hours and were often home during the day. As a matter of fact, I now remember that one of the men who sang for us was a fireman.

The first movie I ever saw was at school and it was called *Geronimo*. I was terrified as I looked up at the screen and saw these savages surrounding the wagon train, and I thought they were going to scalp me. I got down on the floor and covered my eyes. As I said, they were not politically correct in St. Francis.

Monday through Friday we went to school, but on Saturdays, we were off. From about age ten, most of the children were given twelve cents and off to the movies we went. We loved the movies; it was pure escapism watching Cary Grant and Myrna Loy build their dream house, watching Cary Grant and Shirley Temple in the idyllic world of the Bachelor and the Bobby Soxer, watching Clark Gable and Loretta Young in the *Call of the Wild*, and on and on. Many of the movies of that time allowed us to go inside the houses of the upper classes and see how these people lived. We learned manners, how to dress, and how to dance from watching those movies.

The movie theatres always played two movies, an "A" movie and a "B" movie. In addition to the two movies, we saw the newsreels which were called "The Eyes and Ears of the World" plus a serial about Captain Midnight or some other such character. All in all, we could expect to spend four hours in the movies on a Saturday afternoon.

I can remember the first time air-conditioning was introduced to us in movie theatres. It was absolutely freezing, and thereafter you always had to bring a sweater to the movies. But in the sweltering heat of the city summer, we loved it. You could go to the movies at twelve o'clock when it opened and stay as long as you wanted. Every movie theatre had a matron. She was a woman who wore a white uniform and carried a flashlight. She watched the children so that no harm came to them. If they misbehaved, they were thrown out of the theatre. The movies ran continuously all day.

In between the "A" and the "B" movies, we would see "The Eyes and Ears of the World" which gave us some insight into how the war was going. I can vividly recall the newsreel covering the D-Day invasion. It was so real. It showed the young men cramped in the barges preparing to land at Normandy. I can remember being terrified, myself, and wondering how those soldiers jumped into the water and made their way to the beach. We could see that they were being fired upon by the Germans and dying in the water. I kept thinking to myself, "Why don't those men just lie down in the water or on the beach and make believe they are dead until the shooting stops?" Of course, I was just a child and didn't know that the soldiers had no choice but to land and fight. I remember thinking how brave and courageous they were. I believe the landing at Normandy was a lot more horrendous than the newsreel that was shown to the moviegoer. I can't imagine what the mothers and wives of these soldiers thought when they saw the Normandy invasion pictures. Years later I visited Normandy and saw the beaches and cemeteries and thanked God for those brave men. I was moved by the white crosses and stars in the American cemetery as well as the black crosses in the German cemetery. The Normandy cemeteries are stark reminders of the price of freedom and the cost of war.

When my Uncle Chris was drafted into the Navy, he was 32, and the father of a little boy, and we were all shocked, because we thought at age 32 he was too old to be drafted. By this time, my mother and father were proud United States citizens. My Dad said, "We are in it now; just like everyone else." My Uncle Chris ended up on the U.S.S. Ticonderoga, an aircraft carrier, active in the South Pacific. He was in several naval battles, and his ship was hit by a kamikaze. A kamikaze was a Japanese pilot who was on a suicide mission to fly his plane, with him in it, into United States ships to destroy them. I remember that my uncle told us he was ordered up from the engine room where he was stationed to clear bodies off the flight deck after the Ticonderoga was hit by a kamikaze in a battle.

My most vivid remembrance of World War II was the day the Western Union messenger arrived at our apartment building with a telegram for Mr. & Mrs. Bachman. They were our next door neighbors and had an only son who was an Army officer serving in Germany. The war had just ended the day before, and their son, Joe, was killed in a motor vehicle accident. My mother was talking to Mrs. Bachman on the stoop when the fellow arrived with the telegram. Both she and Mrs. Bachman knew intuitively what was in the telegram. Mrs. Bachman took the telegram, went upstairs without saying a word, and everyone knew that Joe Bachman, a tall, handsome, fun loving guy was dead. The whole neighborhood was shocked and a pall came over our block on Bedford

Avenue, and victory celebrations ended. Mr. and Mrs. Bachman immediately went into decline and shortly after, they died. It was the first time I had ever witnessed such sadness.

I remember that during the war years, every family was issued a ration book. A ration book contained stamps which were used to purchase meat and butter. Every time a housewife went to purchase meat or butter, she had to produce her ration book along with the money, and the grocer or butcher would tear out the appropriate number of stamps required for the item. The book was good for a month. At the end of the month, if the housewife didn't have the appropriate stamps, she could not purchase the butter or whatever, until the new book arrived the following month. Ration books were also issued for shoes, as I remember, because leather was essential to the war effort, and the army had first priority on leather for the combat boots. Ration stamps were necessary if one wanted to repair shoes with the shoemaker. He could not repair the shoes without the ration stamps. That was the law, and it was strictly enforced. I can remember my mother putting cardboard in our shoes because she was trying to save the ration coupons for my father's shoes.

The shoemaker's shop was an interesting place. You could sit in a little booth while the shoemaker, who was invariably an Italian, would repair your shoes. We only had one pair of shoes, and you just had to sit and wait for them to be resoled. It was also an interesting place, as friends of the shoemaker would be visiting him, and they all spoke Italian, and he always had an Italian opera playing on his radio. I remember it was the first time I had ever heard the word "opera."

I do remember that there was great excitement in our neighborhood on V-J Day (the day the war with Japan ended). The celebrations for V-E Day were a little bit more subdued because the war was still on and our troops were still not home. But V-J Day was different. Bonfires were burning, toilet paper was being thrown out of windows on Bedford Avenue, pots and pans were banging, and people were dancing in the streets. Everyone stayed up much later that night to celebrate.

There were block parties all over Brooklyn. The street was closed and people came out of their apartments with food, soda and beer to celebrate the end of the war. Music was played and dancing was the order of the day. Ice cream was served to all the children. People spontaneously chipped in what money they could to pay for the ice cream. We celebrated and were immensely relieved. I believe my experiences growing up in this era led me, like many in my generation, to have a permanent fascination for the history of World War II and a great respect for those like my Uncle Chris who fought for their country in its hour of need.

It Only Happens Now and Then ...

The Post War Years

After the war, things settled down, and everyone got on with life. The most crucial thing in our family at that time was the need to find a place for my Uncle Chris and his family to live. When the men came home from the war, housing was at a premium and finding an apartment was almost impossible. By a great piece of luck, an apartment became available in our building, and my uncle and his family moved in. I remember that the apartment needed an enormous amount of work to make it livable, but my uncle and aunt were so glad to get it, that they fixed it up all by themselves.

So now, my Dad and his brother, Uncle Chris, were living in the same building; Chris lived on the fourth floor and we lived on the third. We spent all sorts of time going up and down and socializing with them. Music was a big part of our socializing in those days as we had no television. What we did have was a wonderful radio and phonograph. I remember that it was made by a firm called Stromberg Carlson, and it was a top of the line piece. My Dad was always into buying the best. When my Dad bought something, my uncle bought the same thing, but my uncle bought a piece manufactured by RCA because by this time he was working in the RCA Corporation and he was committed to RCA. These radio consoles were beautiful pieces of furniture that were made of cherry wood and added to the décor of the living room. You could listen to the radio or you could load ten records on the turntable, and they would play for a long time. My parents loved Irish music and Bing Crosby.

Whenever we had friends visiting, my parents would roll back the rug, and they and their friends would do Irish dancing. I have never forgotten what fun that was. When they finished dancing, they would sit around and, one after another, the guests would sing mostly old, sad, lovely Irish songs. My Uncle Chris' favorite was "The Rose of Tralee." I never hear that song without seeing my Uncle Chris with his arm around Peggy singing that song.

My mother was very gay and fun at these parties, and she had a wonderful infectious laugh. One of the things my mother frivolously spent money on was records, usually something by Bing Crosby. Whenever a new Bing Crosby record was released, she would buy it. He was such a part of our life growing up. People don't realize what a favorite Bing Crosby was. I can remember the evening that my Dad came home with his latest recording "Galway Bay." We played that over and over. As I look back on it now, buying those records was a real luxury item, but my parents obviously loved the songs.

While I am reminiscing about the radio, I should say something about how everyone in Brooklyn had a radio, not a television. One thing that stands out in my mind was the night that Joe Louis was fighting Billy Conn. It was a warm night, and all the windows in the apartment houses were open in order to catch a breeze. From any part of the buildings, or if you were walking on the street, you could hear the fight. It seems that everyone in Brooklyn was listening to the fight that night.

In 1950, my Dad bought a new car. He couldn't drive, but he bought a car as soon as he could after the war was over, and then he learned to drive. After he could drive, we went out every Sunday for the traditional "Sunday drive." This was a traumatic experience for my mother, as my Dad always chose to drive on the Grand Central Parkway which my mother kept screaming was a "death trap." It was a winding, treacherous road, and was not the place for a practicing driver with three children and a hysterical wife. In the midst of my mother screaming about our impending death, my Dad continued to smoke his cigar choking us to death. Of course, we kids thought it was fun. What did we know? We thought the Cyclone in Coney Island was fun too.

The next thing we got was a telephone. We had been on the list for a long time, and finally we had a party line. A party line meant that several families were on the one telephone line. If you picked up the phone to make a call, often you would hear someone speaking on the telephone to someone else. If it wasn't an emergency, you just hung up and waited for the phone line to be free. If it was an emergency, you politely asked the person on the line if you could make a call. Most people on a party line were quite civilized and would hang up and allow you to make a call. There was no such thing as a teenager being allowed to talk on the phone for an hour or so. As a matter of fact, the telephone was only used to make important calls such as to the doctor. Social calling on the telephone was not condoned because you were sharing the line with other people and you couldn't tie up the line on frivolous conversation. Before we got the party line, if anyone wanted to call us, they called the candy store on the corner and Mr. Rosen, the Jewish man who owned the candy store, would ring the downstairs bell to our apartment three times, and we would answer. I'm not sure of the details of this arrangement, but Mr. Rosen was very nice to do this for us and other people.

When we got a telephone call, it was usually for my Dad, and it was usually on a Sunday because that was his day off, and something was going amiss in the Hotel

Belvedere, where my Dad was the Superintendent of Service, and he had to settle the problem. He used to say that life was much simpler when we didn't have a telephone and no one could interrupt his Sunday.

I remember the time that my father decided that we were now going to celebrate Thanksgiving "American Style." I think he got into this after seeing my Aunt Peggy set her table for Thanksgiving with its all matching china and crystal. It was so beautiful! All those things were gifts to Peggy and Chris when they married. I believe they were given to them by the priests from the rectory in the parish in the Bronx where she had worked. I think she was a maid there, and she was trained in the proper setting of a table and so forth. In any event, my father and I went downtown to Loser's, and he picked out the china and silver. I don't recall that he bought any crystal, as we had Waterford Crystal because visitors from Ireland always brought gifts to us of Waterford Crystal. From that time on, we always used this china and silver for Thanksgiving, Christmas and Easter. My friends who came to visit always thought we were so civilized. And my mother produced these holiday dinners. Many times my father worked on Christmas because it was a big day for tips in the hotel, but we all waited until he came home around 4 p.m. for our Christmas dinner.

Thinking about Christmas reminds me of a couple of stories. First of all, I, who was hardly ever sick, was always sick during the Christmas vacation. It was unofficially diagnosed as asthma ... which was in those days considered an allergy to something or other. Anyway, because I was sick at Christmas, my mother would always let me sleep in the living room on a couch near the Christmas tree. It turns out that I was allergic to the Christmas tree, and this act of kindness by my mother was almost killing me.

When I went to high school, my mother decided that I was no longer going to sleep on the couch, but in my own room, and after that, I was never sick, thank God. As a matter of fact, I missed only one day of school during my high school years, and that was not because of illness. I was always sorry for taking off that one day from school because when I was graduating, the teachers told me I would have been given a special award for perfect attendance if I hadn't missed that one day. I always felt they should have announced that an award would be given for perfect attendance. If I had known that, I never would have missed a day, especially when I was in my senior year.

My other vivid recollection of Christmas was the year I was about eight years old, right in the middle of the war. Toys were hard to come by, but I really wanted Santa Claus to bring me a "magic skin doll." This was a baby doll that had some type of rubber skin that made it look just like a baby. My mother told me that the war was on and she didn't know if Santa would bring everything I asked for, but I said I had only asked for one thing … the magic skin doll. When I woke up that Christmas not only did Santa leave the magic skin doll, but he also left a beautiful English pram for the doll. It was navy blue. I couldn't believe my eyes. It turned out that my Uncle Chris, who was working in Macy's Department Store at the time, had been on the lookout for the doll and on Christmas Eve he had somehow been able to finally buy one. All the while, my Dad had been saving the doll carriage as a Christmas present for me. A hotel guest had checked out leaving it behind.

Because my Dad worked in the hotel, and it was located right across the street from the old Madison Square Garden, many of the performers who came to New York City for shows in the Garden lived in the Belvedere Hotel during the run of the show. This was a great perk for my family, as the performers knew my father and were always giving him free tickets to the shows. These were house tickets, so they were always good seats. My brothers and I, and often our friends, would go to New York with my Mom, meet my Dad at the hotel, and go to see the shows.

If we were going into the city to meet my father, we had to be dressed properly. He did not want us appearing at "his" hotel dressed like ragamuffins. We always wore our Sunday clothes when we went to New York to see my father. He was very proud of us and my mother and he always introduced us to everyone who came down into the lobby where his desk was.

Once, we met Roy Rogers, the famous cowboy, who came to New York with the rodeo. I loved to see the cowgirls and cowboys who congregated around the lobby before the show. The trick riders wore lavish sequined costumes, both the men and women, and to me, they were all so glamorous.

One of my most vivid memories was the time I saw Sonja Henie, the world famous ice skater. She had an ice skating show that was touring the country, and when she came to the Garden, we had tickets. I can remember being in the Garden, and all the lights were down, except for a spotlight which was shining on a box in the middle of the arena. It was a big box, standing on its end, covered in cellophane. It was the type of box a doll came in. And there was a doll inside the box. As I watched the box, the doll came to life and began to wrap on the cellophane, and then the cellophane broke, and out stepped what looked to me like an ice skating doll. She was so beautiful. She had on this wonderful pink costume with fur, and she began to dance around. Of course, it was Sonja Henie. She gave a breathtaking performance, and that Christmas, Santa Claus left me an authentic Sonja Henie doll.

Speaking of ice skating, I want to tell another story. In our apartment, in my brothers' room, there was a closet with two big drawers at the bottom of it. These drawers were full of ice skates in a variety of sizes. There were figure skates and hockey skates. All these skates came from my Dad's hotel, and they were all given to him by the people in the skating show. They didn't need them anymore so they gave them to my father for his kids. We were the only children in the neighborhood who had ice skates. They were a luxury item, and most people were lucky to have shoes, and money was not spent frivolously on ice skates. Anyway, all of our friends had access to these drawers, and if they could find a pair of skates that fit them, they could have them.

Naturally, my friend Betty found a pair that fit her, and I had a pair that fit me. Where to skate was the question? At the back of the church grounds, there was a big quadrangle where the students from Brooklyn Prep played basketball. In the winter it wasn't used and when it snowed or rained, the water froze and it made a perfect skating rink. Of course, we were not supposed to go into the quadrangle, and it was locked every evening, but the gate didn't fully close and a slim child could squeeze through it. Betty and I and my brother Tom would sneak into the quadrangle at about five in the evening when no one could see us and skate to our hearts content.

One evening, when Betty tried to squeeze through the gate (it was closed tighter than usual) she got her head stuck inside the fence and her body outside the fence. There was no way we could get her out so we had to call the priest and ask him to come out and open the lock on the gate. He wasn't happy about it, and forbid us to ever skate there again. We then decided to skate in Prospect Park which was quite a distance away, but we did it.

We would come home, get our skates and walk about a mile to the park. We would stay there in the dark, skating on the lake. In the boathouse, there was a potbellied stove, and we could go in there to warm our gloves and put our skates on and off. You could also buy a hot chocolate if you had a dime. As I look back on it, it was amazing that our mothers would let us do this. Their only order was that we be home by six o'clock for dinner. They didn't seem to be worried that we would be attacked or kidnapped or frozen to death in the park or fall through the ice. Naturally, the lake had flags on it to tell you if you could skate, and we obeyed them.

On one of our trips to the city, we saw the world famous Ringling Brothers Barnum & Bailey Circus. My Dad introduced us to the giant and his wife who was also a giant. They were over eight feet tall, and my father said that they slept in separate beds and that to accommodate them they pushed single beds end to end to make a bed long enough for them to sleep in. We met midgets who were in the circus, and many other performers. Whatever event came to Madison Square Garden, we saw it, and the seats were always great. We thought everyone did this when they were little; we didn't understand what a great experience it was to be able to attend all these events. We had a culturally enriched childhood thanks to my father's great personality.

There was another unusual perk of my father's job that I remember. Whenever the rodeo was in town, and the cowboys were in from Texas, they always tipped my father in silver dollars. My Dad saved these and whenever any child came to visit us on Sundays, he or she went home with a silver dollar. I think it was an Irish custom to give coins to visiting children. No child ever left our house without a silver dollar in his pocket. These silver dollars also figured in a story I will save for later.

While I am on the subject of going to New York, I want to mention also that my Dad often received tickets to Broadway theatre shows from guests who lived in the hotel permanently. These guests were the actors and actresses that worked in the theatres. Since my mother did not like to go to New York, when I was about fourteen, and could ride on the subway alone, I travelled to the city to go to the theatre with my father. I can remember his taking me to a real French restaurant … it was the first time I was ever in a French restaurant, and we had a great time. The maître d' knew my father and treated us very special. In the area of 48th street and 8th avenue, there were loads of restaurants, and I think my Dad knew everyone who owned a restaurant because this was his neighborhood, and he knew everyone in it. My Dad worked at the Hotel Belvedere his whole life until he was 65. One day I asked him if he ever regretted leaving Ireland to come to the United States and he said, "No, I loved it here. I had a most interesting life, I met all sorts of interesting people in the hotel business, and I never regretted the decision I made."

Days, weeks and years passed, and our childhood was without incident other than a few whacks given to us by our parents for misbehaving. Exactly how we were misbehaving I can't remember unless it was being late for dinner. We never "talked back" to our parents. It just wasn't tolerated.

Summers were spent going to summer school which was like a camp run by our parish. All the Catholic children went to summer school every morning at nine and did organized fun activities until twelve noon when the city of Brooklyn delivered free lunches for everyone. This sounds like something that was done for poor people, but we had no idea we were poor. We thought everyone got a free lunch in Brooklyn. On Wednesday in the summer, buses came to our summer school and took us on a beach outing, either to Rockaway Beach or to Coney Island. All of this was free, including the lunch, and even the facilities of a bathhouse. There was a very generous man in Brooklyn at the time named Dave Soden, and he sponsored these trips. All of these things were to keep us "off the mean streets" and they worked.

On the days when summer school was over at noon, my friend, Betty, and I would go to Girls' Commercial High School for swimming lessons. This was a public school, and it was open to the children of the neighborhood to cool them off on hot summer afternoons. The sessions were about 40 minutes each, and Betty and I would get on line, go to the first session, and then go outside and wait for the next session. Usually, we spent an hour and half there, and we learned how to swim and dive in that pool. Everything was free.

At the end of the summer, the biggest treat of all was a trip to Steeplechase Park. This was a great amusement park in Coney Island, and we were each given a round ticket that hung on a string which was attached to our clothing, and we could go on any ride we wanted. What a thrill; we loved it. Our family went to Steeplechase twice during the summer, once with summer school and once with my mother. She would take us and some of our friends for a day at Steeplechase. We could go on the rides all day and she would sit on a park bench, all dressed up with a hat on (she was very fair skinned and hated to get sunburned) and just "be there" in this one spot in case we needed to find her. Other than that, we were allowed to roam at free will through the amusement park. Of course, the park was all fenced in so she wasn't afraid we would get lost or anything like that. In those days, in Brooklyn, no one kidnapped children.

In the middle of August every year, our whole family went to a boarding house in Liberty, New York. This boarding house was run by a farmer and his wife, and it was a full working farm with cows, bulls, chickens, hayrides, etc. It was a monumental task for my mother to wash and iron all our clothes for a two-week stay on a farm. She had no washing machine. While we were in summer school, she would be getting ready for this trip. I'm sure it took at least two weeks to wash, iron and pack several suitcases for this excursion. My Dad was adamant about our going on vacation every year. He loved the country and the farm, as it reminded him of Ireland. Almost every summer, we extended our trip to three weeks because we were having such a good time, and it was so hot in the city that my Dad left us for another week while he went back to the sweltering city. We did this trip all through the war years.

I can remember my parents lugging suitcases into the subway and then into the Dixie Bus Terminal where we would take the Greyhound Bus. Riding the Greyhound was a great luxury for us. What an ordeal that must have been for my parents … traveling with three kids and about four large suitcases. When the bus arrived at Liberty, New York, we were met at the bus stop by the owner of the boarding house and went by car the rest of the way.

During these vacations, my mother and father's friends would join us, and the whole boarding house would be filled with congenial Irish people who loved to sing and dance. My brothers and I spent our days visiting the barn to watch the cows being milked, watching the lady of the house strangle the chickens which were cooked for Sunday and Wednesday dinner, watching the farmer bale hay, getting rides on the hay wagon, and, mostly, swimming in a pond that was on the property. In the evenings, everyone would walk to town, a distance of two miles, have an ice cream and walk back in the dark. By that time all the children were tired, put to bed, and the adults got together in an out building called the "Wigwam" for dancing and drinks. There was something for everyone at the boarding house.

The big thing for my mother was that she didn't have to shop or prepare a meal for two, sometimes three, weeks, and she was very happy about that. My Dad felt it was important that my mother have a real vacation away from the stove. The life of a wife and mother in Brooklyn entailed shopping every day for food, and in my mother's case, lugging it up three stories to our apartment. Countless bottles of milk, pounds of potatoes and vegetables, and all the stuff to keep a family fed. It was a hard job and no wonder my mother needed a break.

Summers in the city were very hot, and most people in apartment houses, when supper was over, would go down to the stoop to socialize. A stoop was a set of stairs at the entrance to the apartment building. People would congregate on the stoops in the evening for a smoke and a chat while the children played on the sidewalk. Since we lived up the block from Ebbets Field, the home of the famous Brooklyn Dodgers, we were treated many nights to the sight of all the fans coming down our block from the subway station heading to Ebbets Field for a night game. It was very exciting. The avenue was full of great cars coming from Bedford Stuyvesant, the black neighborhood, to the game. Black people were great baseball fans and while I was young there was not a black player on the Dodger's baseball team, but still the black people were fans. They would go to the games all dressed up: shirts, ties and hats for the men and beautiful dresses and high heels for the women. They were very stylish and fun loving people. During my teen years, Jackie Robinson, the famous black baseball player was introduced to major league baseball, and the team that hired him was the Brooklyn Dodgers. It was a momentous occasion for all baseball, and we lived two blocks away from where it happened.

Baseball was a major part of the life of everyone who lived in Brooklyn. My mother was an avid Dodger fan and listened to the games all the time. I can remember coming home from school at 3:30 and she would have the baseball game on the radio. She went to Ebbets Field for afternoon games on Ladies' Day when she could get into the field for 25 cents.

The organist who played for all the Dodger games lived in my Dad's hotel. Her name was Gladys Gooding, and she was quite famous … at least she was famous in Brooklyn. She had an overhanging box right over first base from where she played the organ, and she was always inviting us down to the game. This was another perk of my father's job.

In 1947, right after the war ended, and people were able to travel on commercial airlines, my father purchased a ticket on Trans World Airlines to go to Shannon, Ireland. My Dad always longed to return to Waterford to see his mother and family, but World War II prevented that. It took twelve hours to cross the Atlantic at that time. There was great excitement in our apartment getting my Dad ready for the trip. Presents had to be bought for all his brothers and sisters, and since there were twelve of them living in Ireland, plus his mother, it was a major task to assemble all these gifts keeping in mind that the luggage was weighed and could not exceed a certain amount. It was such a novelty in those days to fly that a large contingent of friends went to the airport to see him off, and when he returned he told us great stories of how so many of his brothers and sisters met him at the airport and what a great time they had stopping at various pubs along the way on their trip back to Waterford. That trip was the highlight of his life. Everyone was so happy to see him, and he was entertained in the most wonderful fashion. He had a great love for his family and always spoke with great pride about them.

Even though he was going on a three-week vacation to Ireland, he didn't forget us in the hot city, and made plans for us to go to Cairo, New York, which was an Irish enclave in the Catskills. This time we travelled on the

Hudson River Day Line which was a boat that left from a pier on 42nd street in Manhattan, and travelled up the Hudson River to its destination.

My brother, Tom, was fifteen at the time, and had acquired a second hand bike that was painted completely black due to its use in blackouts during the war. He wanted to take it on the vacation so he would have some mode of transportation when we got to the country. He rode the bike through Brooklyn, over the Manhattan Bridge, and all the way to 42nd Street so that he could put the bike on the boat. It was quite an adventure for a fifteen year old boy.

I remember that we never went to Cairo again, as my mother felt it was "too Irish" for her, meaning too much drinking. My mother was a woman with strong opinions. I will devote a chapter to my mother as the memoir goes on, but I do want to say that I am so grateful to my parents for getting us out of the hot muggy city with these trips to the country. It took a lot of effort and money for them to do that for us.

Another summer story that I recall pertains to my brother Tom, and the gang of neighborhood boys that he had in his club. The club would meet in the basement of our apartment house, and they collected dues. There were about eight boys in this club. They were Norwegian, Irish, Jewish, Greek … a real melting pot of kids. This all took place during World War II around 1944. These boys all had little jobs such as delivering newspapers or groceries, and running errands for elderly people in the neighborhood, and they saved up their money. When they had enough money saved they went to an Army Navy store where they could buy surplus army equipment They bought knapsacks, utensils (knife, fork, spoon, dish

… all aluminum) like the soldiers had, a canteen for each boy and a cartridge belt on which to carry this equipment. Included in their purchases were army blankets which they used in place of sleeping bags. They also bought two inflatable rafts each of which held five men.

The boys would all gather on the corner near our building at about 7:30 on a Saturday morning. They would take the subway to the 181st Street station in Manhattan and then walk across the George Washington Bridge to reach New Jersey. From there they would hike up Route 9W about 3 miles to a small town name Coytesville where there was a quarry. They would set up camp at the quarry and would hike around for a couple of hours exploring. Eventually, they would make a camp fire and cook whatever food they brought with them … usually hot dogs and beans. After eating, they would pack up and start back on the journey down Route 9W, across the bridge, back on the subway, arriving home around 8:30 in the evening. All the parents would be sitting on the stoops of the apartment house waiting for their return. I am sure the parents were somewhat anxious as this was a great adventure for these boys who were very young and not used to outdoor living. Tom was the leader of the pack, and he was about twelve when this "troop" got started. The other boys were about eight or ten years of age. Tom recalls that once they stayed overnight in the quarry, but in the beginning most of the trips were just day hikes.

When Tom was fourteen but before he went to high school, the "club" decided to go on a real two or three day hike. They planned to do this over the Easter vacation, and they saved up their money for this special trip. Tom says that he thinks the boys' mothers (not their fathers) gave them some money for this trip. (I think mothers always want their sons to have some adventure in their lives.) Tom planned the trip using maps that he had gotten from the Palisades Park Commission. The boys wanted to use their rafts and so it was decided that they would have to travel as far as the Red Apple Rest, a bus stop for the Trailways bus company, which was situated on Route 17 North near the Ramapo River. For this trip, they had to take the subway to 42nd Street in Manhattan to where the bus depot was located at the Dixie Hotel. There was no Port of Authority Bus Terminal in those days. It took two boys to carry one raft so it was quite a chore getting these rafts to New York City. Two boys put the raft on a pole and carried it over their shoulders. When they got to the bus depot, they put their gear and the rafts in the luggage section of the Trailways bus and traveled to the town of Southfields where the Red Apple Rest was located. They then proceeded through the parking lot at the back of the Red Apple Rest and down a trail which was behind the lot until they got to the Ramapo River. I asked Tom how he knew all this "stuff" coming from Brooklyn, and he told me he just used maps. I have always been impressed with Tom's knowledge of maps and his great ability to figure things out on his own. When they got to the river, they launched the rafts. Each raft had four boys in it. It's amazing when you think about it. They had no life jackets and only a 14 year old boy to guide them.

Their ultimate destination was Tuxedo, New York, and they made it, but not without a little extra adventure. It seems that someone shot at them with a 22 rifle from the woods while they were on their rafts in the river. The bullet pierced the inflatable seat that one of the boys was sitting on, just missing his backside. The raft did not sink because it was compartmentalized. Tom said there was no reason to shoot at them … just some lunatic in the woods probably "having fun."

They camped in Tuxedo for about 2 or 3 days and just wandered around hiking in the woods. It was a great adventure. Camping in the woods in the springtime can be very cold especially when all you have to sleep in is an army blanket, but there were no sleeping bags for these guys. Tom said no one actually told their parents what the plans were, especially about the rafting on the river, but no one's parents objected to the boys having a little adventure. They were out of communications for about 3 days. Just think about it … these were the days before cell phones and there were very few public phones so you were really on your own out there in the woods. Tom said he knows my mother was praying that they would return safely and they did. I don't believe my father ever worried about Tom. He knew that he was a trustworthy, smart guy.

Joseph never went on these outings because he was a little too young and by the time he was ready to go hiking he was in the Boy Scout troop which my Dad helped organize in our parish. As I look back on it now, I think my Dad got involved in the Boy Scouts because he saw how much fun Tom and the other kids had had when they went hiking.

Now, I'll get back to my main story. I did not have a lot of great adventures like my brother, but I do remember one time when I was about twelve and my friend, Betty, and I went to Coney Island for the day swimming. While we were in the water someone stole my sandals, and I had no shoes to get home. So Betty and I searched through a garbage can, found some cardboard and string, and we made me a pair of sandals so that I could get on the subway. In those days the subway was five cents, and when we went to Coney Island, we always had a quarter … five cents was for the ride home, and the other 20 cents was for a Nathan's hot dog, the best hot dog in the whole world, and an order of French fries, also the best in the world. That was a regular routine for Betty and me. On the way home from the beach we always bought a hot dog and an order of French fries.

I suppose you are wondering where we got the 25 cents to begin with. Every time you bought a large bottle of soda, there was a five cent deposit on the bottle. That meant if you returned the bottle to the store, the grocer would give you five cents. So that's how we did it … we would gather up a few bottles left over from the weekend's entertaining, and turn them in for the cash. Our parents had no problem with this. It gave them a chance to give us some money in return for a little work.

When I was young, everything liquid came in a bottle … milk, cream, soda, etc. When you bought a bottle of milk, and milk was only sold in quart bottles, there was always an inch or two of cream at the top. This we used for our oatmeal in the mornings. I believe that there was deposit money on milk bottles too.

I remember that my mother always used a large Hoffman ginger ale bottle as a rolling pin when she was making her delicious apple pie. This was the dessert of choice in our house. My mother's apple pie was the best. Actually, it was really an apple tart, that is, it was just made with apples and sugar. The smell of this pie baking was fantastic, and it usually appeared on the table for Sunday dinner and all "state occasions," as my mother would say.

57

That meant that special people were coming to dinner. My mother never baked a cake – the apple tart was her specialty (see appendix for recipe). She would use seven green apples and a cup of sugar, and she would roll out the pastry using a large ginger ale bottle. She never had a pastry roller, and didn't see any need to get one when a bottle would do the job. The pie was always served hot with ice cream. As soon as it was time for dessert, my mother would give us some money and we would run downstairs to the candy store and buy a pint of hand-packed vanilla ice cream. In those days, there were no freezers so you could not store ice cream and produce it any time you wanted it. We were so lucky that the ice cream was available to us just by running down the stairs, and going to Mr. Rosen's candy store. He would always say to us, "So your mother baked a pie for you today."

In the country when I was fourteen years old in 1949

It Only Happens Now and Then ...

Teenage Years

Years went by, and finally, I went to high school -- Bishop McDonnell High School for girls. Here I met most of the friends I have 60 years later. There was something about that school that instilled in girls a great feeling of self-worth and camaraderie. We were given a superb education, equal I would say to a college education today. Several orders of Catholic nuns taught at Bishop's. Each order had a specialty. For instance, Dominican nuns taught math and sciences; Mercy nuns taught music and library science; Josephite nuns taught English and Latin, Spanish and Italian; Sisters of Charity taught history and social sciences and the Sisters of Notre Dame taught French. All of these nuns were super bright and devoted to the job of making upstanding women out of their "Bishop's girls." Their demeanor was wonderful, as they flew around the corridors of Bishop's in their various habits maintaining discipline and order. The nuns were all so different from one another. I think their personalities reflected their orders. Some were carefree and gay, and some were aloof and strict, but they were all wonderful women devoted to their calling. Moral values and a deep sense of religion were instilled in Bishop's girls and the qualities have lasted a lifetime and sustained my friends and me through the various ups and downs of life. We all have a deep faith, a gift which was given to us by our parents, and nurtured by these fine teachers.

Bishop McDonnell's was located about five blocks from my house, and it was a scholarship school for the girls from the diocese of Brooklyn. Every parish in Brooklyn was given a specific number of scholarships, depending on the size of the parish, and my parish, St. Ignatius, had one scholarship allotted to it. My dearest friend, Betty Keane, whom I have known since kindergarten, and I were both going for the scholarship, but I was fortunate to get it. Although Betty didn't go to Bishop's with me, she became one of the "Bishop's Crowd" because she always hung around with me and my friends.

When I entered Bishop's I didn't know anyone, but I looked upon it as a great adventure. I loved meeting new people, and I was so fortunate to meet girls who became my lifelong friends. I remember my first day at Bishop's. I didn't know a soul, and all freshmen were assembled in the gym for orientation. When I was in there, I made an instant decision to look around at all the girls, and try to find someone who would be my friend. I saw Anne White, and she was laughing, and she looked like such a fun girl. Somehow I managed to meet Anne even though she was with four other girls she had known from grammar school. It was my good fortune to become her friend, and I have known Anne for over sixty years, and she still is funny. She had a great Irish wit, and together, we were always able to make one another laugh.

After the freshman year, all the students were given an IQ test, and the students with the best scores on this test were put into the "French group." I had no idea we were taking an IQ test, and I was just sitting there fooling around and taking the test at the same time. If I had known how important this test was, I might have paid more attention to it because scoring high on this test had a great impact on my life. Thank God I got a good score. As a result of the grade, I was placed in the "French Group." This was a group of about twenty-two students chosen from about two hundred twenty students to take three years of French as well as four years of Latin. All the girls in this group were very sharp and quick witted. Most of them were Irish, and one of them was Italian. As I said, there were twenty-two of us in the class, and about eight of us were great friends. We spent the last three years of high school together so we became quite close. I am still in contact with my "crowd" over sixty years later.

I can remember when I met these girls that I looked in the mirror one day and did an analysis of my looks. I decided that I was definitely not the best looking girl in this group, and if I ever wanted to be noticed, I had better develop my personality. So that is just what I did. How I did it I don't know, but I was quick witted and that helped me immensely. People just thought I was funny and wanted to hang around with me. And it didn't hurt to hang around with other girls who were quick witted. Every girl in our crowd had a great personality. We were not wildly popular with boys, but everyone else thought we were great fun. In our crowd, one of the things we never did was talk about one another. To this day, we have never done this, and I think that is why we are all friends.

As I said, one of the girls, Annette DeGaetano, was Italian, and when she heard that we had never had Italian food, she invited the seven of us in the crowd to her house for a real Italian dinner. Actually, most of us had had Italian food, or so we thought. Our Irish mothers would make us something called Chef Boyardee. This was an "Italian Dinner" that came complete in a box which contained some spaghetti and a can of tomato sauce. This served our whole family because my Mom and Dad would never eat "Italian." When we went to Annette's house for dinner, never in our lives had we seen such food. When Annette's mother passed around the spaghetti in a soup bowl, I took a portion of it and passed it on to my right. Her mother was horrified, as each girl was to get her own soup bowl of spaghetti. In Italian families, this was a portion for one person. We could never eat the amount of food that was put before us. After the spaghetti course came the chicken and then roast beef and then a great assortment of desserts. It was an experience I have never forgotten.

For the next three years of school, the eight of us palled around. Our "clique" (that's what other girls in Bishop's called us) consisted of Dolores Bryan, Annette DeGaetano, Theresa Donahue, Bobby McCarthy, Ann White, Helen Kernaghan, as well as Peg Casella & Betty Keane (who were not in the French group, but were just "in" with us) and me. After school, we went to a soda shop called Karp's, and sat there for an hour laughing and giggling. We were frivolous individuals, and it was a care-free time. We were waiting to "grow up."

Mentioning the soda shop reminds me of a favorite person during my teenage years. It was a fellow by the name of Matty Parker. He was the first boy I ever really went out on a date with. He always hung around Karp's Soda Shop, but I actually met him at a local parish dance. He was the most marvelous dancer, and handsome and charming. He asked me to dance because he knew I was a great dancer, and he wanted someone who could follow him. He did not dance in the conventional way … he was amazingly creative and no two steps of his were alike, but he had difficulty finding someone who could dance with him. When he found out I could do it, I became his dancing partner. When I met him I was a junior in high school, and I had never been on a date. My Dad always maintained it would be time for dating, and wearing makeup, etc., when I was eighteen. Nevertheless, Bishop McDonnell was holding a big dance, and all my friends were going and they wanted me to go. In those days, if a girl's school was having the dance, the girl had to ask the boy to the dance. I finally got the courage to ask Matty to go with me, and he was delighted to go. I was thrilled. My mother made me a beautiful teal blue velvet dress; my brother Tom took my friend Anne White (she didn't have a boyfriend either); my Dad gave Tom the car and off we went. When we arrived at the dance, my friends from school were surprised at what a great looking boy friend I had arrived with, and when they saw him dance, they were amazed. It was a great night, and we all had a wonderful time, especially me. It was such fun to dance around with Matty. I never seriously considered him as a potential suitor, as he came from a strange family, and he lived in a fantasy world. He had difficulty separating fact from fiction. While he might have been a marvelous dancer, a terrific storyteller, and a great looking guy, I knew he wasn't for me. We always stayed great friends. And as a matter of fact, he was going to take me to my Senior Prom, but he did not have the money, as it was very expensive to do this, so instead he and Betty and I sat in Karp's and he treated us to an ice cream soda the night of the prom. I didn't miss going to the prom because he was so kind and nice. Years later he married a dear friend of mine. They lived in a brownstone house in the Park Slope section of Brooklyn. It was a beautiful townhouse, and he and his wife fixed it up to look like a New York townhouse. They were one of the first people to realize the potential of buying a house in Park Slope. I believe they paid $18,000 for the house, and today it is worth over a million dollars. Unfortunately, Matty developed a major drinking problem which caused the breakup of his marriage. To his credit, he overcame his problem and went on to live a productive life.

Years later, in October 2001, while I was preparing to go to Germany to visit my son, the phone rang, and Matty Parker was calling me. I remember the call so clearly, as he was very ill and dying and he called to say how much he had always loved me, and to thank me for being so kind to him. I was very moved by this call, and told him I would be in touch with him when we returned from Europe. When I got around to calling him, he had passed away. He was a very kind and gentle man.

As I mentioned earlier he had had a sad life. His parents were abusive, and treated him and his brother and two sisters very badly. They always wore hand-me-down clothes, and they were never properly cared for. As a result of his childhood, Matty always lived in a dream world. That is where he developed his habit of telling "tall tales." He was a marvelous story teller and could make everyone laugh. Because he never had any nice clothes or anything like that, when he began to work, he only shopped in the best stores. He was especially fussy about his shoes and after he started working he only wore the most beautiful footwear. As a child his mother always bought him shoes from the bargain basement, and he hated that. It was the loss of his shoes one night on the subway that helped him get over his drinking problem. On his ride home, he had fallen asleep after too many drinks and he woke to find that someone had stolen his shoes. He was so shocked over the loss of a great pair of shoes and the fact that he had to walk home from the subway barefoot that he decided to give up drinking. When Matty was about twenty-one, he married Bobbie and took his siblings away from his parents. He and Bobbie helped raise them and did a pretty good job.

All the girls in my Bishop's crowd went to college except me. The girls in Bishop McDonnell's were never encouraged to go to a public college. That was unfortunate because all the girls in the French group were college material, but we all didn't have the money for private colleges. If we had been encouraged to go to public colleges, like Brooklyn College or Hunter, we probably would have gone, as it would not have been a problem scholastically. We were all directed to private Catholic colleges, and the girls who did go worked very hard to pay their tuition at these private institutions. I had no interest in going to college, because it was expensive, and my Dad didn't consider it important that I go to college. He was only interested in sending my brothers to college. That was pretty much the way it was in those days. Sons went to college and daughters got married. No one ever assumed that their daughter wouldn't get married. I had no interest in going to college, because I didn't like school. It was easy and no problem, but I just didn't like it. On the last day of high school, I burned all my books in a tin garbage pail which was outside of the school. It was an act of defiance.

It Only Happens Now and Then …

.

Work and Life in the 1950s

So ... I went to work. My Dad would have sent me to college if I knew what I wanted to be. In those days, a girl could be a school teacher or a nurse. I didn't want to be either of those, so my Dad said I should get a job. I was going to go to nursing school in September because it was something to do, but it interfered with my Dad's vacation which was the last three weeks of August.

Before I get into the story of this vacation, I have to tell the story of how my Dad bought this huge pink piggy bank, and every night when he came home from work he put all his loose change in the pig. He only put silver in the pig, fifty-cent pieces, quarters, nickels and dimes. This money came from the tips he made during the day. When this bank was full, he was going to spend it on a great vacation. After months of saving, the day came when we were going to break open the pig. We put newspapers on the dining room table, put the big pig on the table, and cracked it open with a hammer. Out rushed all these coins, and just then, the doorbell rang. My mother answered the door, and it was a friend of theirs from Ireland, whose ship had just docked (he was a merchant seaman), and he had just stopped by to visit. My mother was dumbfounded to see him, and of course, she invited him in. When he came into the dining room and saw all the money on the table, he said, "So it is true. The streets are paved with gold in America!" We all laughed at that and invited him to sit down and "start counting." There was over $500.00 in that pig and so we were ready to go on a vacation.

My Dad had decided to go on a long motor trip to Canada, and he wanted me to go. He told me to call up the nursing school and tell them I wasn't coming, and I did because I wasn't sure I wanted to be a nurse anyway. My father's reaction to my being a nurse was that he didn't want me emptying bed pans. And so, we all went off on our family vacation to Quebec and Montreal … my career in nursing left behind.

After our vacation, I started a job with New York Life Insurance Co. in the actuarial department. They had given me a test when they hired me and ascertained that I had an aptitude for figures. I think they were grooming me for one day being the head of the actuarial department, as they seated me in the very front right near the boss, and ahead of everyone in the room. I was there six months when I looked around and all I could see were "women." I decided this was not good for my career which I had determined was going to be a wife and mother. There were no men in the New York Life actuarial department, and I decided I was going to get out of there.

I asked my father about going to secretarial school, and now that I had a goal in mind, he had no problem paying my tuition. I went to Katharine Gibbs which was the best secretarial school in New York City. Before I could get into this school, I had to go for an interview and my father went with me. Normally, one's mother would have done this because fathers had to work. But he was great. He took off from his job, put on his good suit and met me at 230 Park Avenue for the interview. My father had great confidence and going to an interview on Park Avenue didn't bother him at all. Of course, the admissions director found him charming, as I knew she would, and I was "in." I loved it.

I was a born secretary. I never regretted for one minute my decision not to go to college. Secretarial school was the perfect place for me. I did well there, and, afterward, I got my first secretarial job in the advertising department of the firm that sold Martex towels.

I started in the advertising department because I took a personality test which told them, that I was creative, and it turned out that I was. I could draw and I had a good sense of fashion and color, and I was able to speak to buyers and fashion editors who came into the showroom to see the towels. It was a fun job. I have been very fortunate in my jobs. I only had two jobs before I married and both of them were very interesting.

The best thing that happened at Martex was that I met my future husband. Before I get into the details of my courtship, I will write a few things about my life as a single gal growing up in Brooklyn.

As soon as I got my first job, I decided to do something I had been thinking about for a long time. I decided to get braces on my teeth. My teeth were crooked, and this bothered me. It didn't bother my parents ... they thought I looked fine. I took myself to an orthodontist that my friend, Marie McCarthy, went to. The McCarthy's were my most sophisticated friends and they all had their teeth straightened. This was a very expensive procedure, but I decided to spend my money on it. It didn't seem to bother me that I was the only grown-up person I had ever seen, at that time, with braces. My Dad thought this was a stupid idea, but if I wanted to spend my money on it, that was my decision. It took two years to straighten my teeth, and it curtailed my social life somewhat, but it was worth it.

When it was finished, I was 20, and that summer I took four weeks off from my job, and went on a trip to Ireland and to Europe. I travelled alone on the plane, an unheard of adventure in my circle of friends. The trip, in a propeller plane, took about eleven hours to Shannon, Ireland. Here I was met by my brother, Tom, who was stationed with the army in Germany. He had decided to visit Ireland to meet all the cousins he had heard about, and my mother thought it would be a good idea if I did some traveling. My mother did have an adventuresome nature, and she wanted me to see some of the world before I married. My trip to Ireland was a highlight of my life. My brother and I met all our first cousins in Waterford, there were about 50 of them, one nicer than the other. They couldn't do enough for us. Irish hospitality was amazing. When we got to my Uncle Joe Carey's house where we would be staying, there were so many Careys and Fitz's there that we were overwhelmed. After we rested one night, we began to go out touring around. Every day we would see the sights, and every night we went dancing until two in the morning. It didn't seem to bother my Irish cousins that they were out all night dancing. They always got up for work the next morning. They were such marvelous people, and we have such fond memories of them.

I remember one night we went to a party at my Aunt Nancy's house, and all my uncles, aunts and older cousins were there. We were doing Irish set dancing in the living room. There was a fiddle player standing on a chair, above the fray, calling the dance. My Uncle Maurice who was a giant of a man (at least 6 feet 4 inches) didn't like the way he was calling the dance, so he picked the fiddler up by the collar, took him off the chair, and took over the calling of the dance. Everybody laughed, and nobody minded the fact that Maurice took over. It was a sight to see.

Tom and I stayed in Ireland for about two weeks. We were staying with my Uncle Joe Carey, who lived with his wife (they had no children) in the beautiful little house where my mother was born at a spot called Holy Cross. We had to take sponge baths because they had no plumbing in the house. They had a chemical toilet in an outhouse. All personal bathing was done in the bedroom with a pitcher of water and a basin. It was amazing to me how my Aunt Kitty, Uncle Joe's wife, could keep her house so sparkling without running water, but she was a marvelous housekeeper. The house literally sparkled. On top of her mantelpiece, she had about sixteen brass candlesticks, and she polished them religiously once a week. She did all her sheets and towels herself, and I think everyday something was hanging on the line or somewhere in the house drying, but it never seemed to disrupt the order of her house.

Anyway, one day my Aunt Nancy, who had a house in town with all the amenities, running water, etc., invited me to town to take a "real bath." I was so happy because I could wash my hair. The funny thing was, when I went upstairs to take the bath, the water was cold. I could not get in the tub, so I just put my hand in there and swished it around so my aunt would think I was taking a bath. What the Irish people thought of as warm water was not what I was used to. Irish people seemed to be impervious to the cold. When I came out of the bathroom, I thanked my Aunt Nancy for going to all the trouble to prepare the bath for me. At the time, she had four young children and was expecting her 5th child. I never realized how much trouble it was to invite her American niece into her house for a bath until after I was married and had my own young children. She was such a nice person, as were all my Irish relations.

For instance, my Aunt Eily, my father's oldest sister, just took us under her wing. She was in charge of arranging that we meet all my father's brothers and sisters and their families. Every day we set out with Aunt Eily in her little car. She was about 60 years old when we met her, a five foot bundle of energy and charm. She drove this little car and on the front of it hanging off the hood ornament was a steel tea kettle. My brother and I never asked her what the kettle was for, as we didn't want to appear nosy. But we found out one afternoon as the little car was climbing up a hill. It began to sputter and steam began to pour out of the radiator. No problem for my Aunt Eily. She just jumped out of the car, opened the hood and poured water from the tea kettle into the radiator. She told us that always happened and that she always carried a tea kettle full of water with her when she went out in her car. At that time, she was one of the few women in Ireland who drove a car, and everyone knew her and her car with the tea kettle on the hood ornament.

Another interesting experience I had in Ireland was the day I went to visit my Aunt Baw. She was the youngest of my father's siblings, and he was particularly fond of her, as she was always with him when he was working on the farm. He said she was like a little pet. She was now married to what I would describe as a "wild Irish man." They lived with their four sons and two daughters on the top of a hill. To get to their house, you had to drive up a narrow lane (there was just room for a car) which was overgrown with wild bushes. When you got up to the top of the lane, there was this old farmhouse. When we went inside the house, it reminded me of Wuthering Heights. It was dark and old. Not only was the house like Wuthering Heights, her husband, a dark brooding Irishman, looked like Heathcliff. But my Aunt Baw was lovely; she was all ready to entertain her brother's children, and she had a beautiful table set with all the things for tea. She had baked all sorts of goodies. She must have been baking all day to put out such a spread. When it came time to make the tea, she had a kettle in the fireplace over an open fire. When the kettle boiled, she just put a piece of newspaper around the handle and removed it from the fire. I was fascinated that she didn't burn her hand … no potholders for her. If I had attempted this maneuver, I would have ended up in the emergency room with a third degree burn. She was a true farmer's wife … a lovely person.

Every place we went in Ireland, we had tea. Tea consisted of great homemade baked goodies, plus little finger sandwiches and, of course, tea. This was all set up with lovely linens and china tea services. It is a ritual of entertaining in Ireland, and it's impossible to refuse the gracious hospitality of these people. My brother and I thought we were going to explode from so much tea.

When our vacation came to an end and we were leaving Waterford, so many people came to the train to see us off, you would think they had known us forever. They were saying their "Irish Goodbyes" which take forever, and the train was just sitting in the station. Finally, the conductor said, "Are ye all through saying goodbye?" Then he closed the doors. In those days, in Ireland, the train schedule was a very casual affair. No one would just slam a door and take off. As a last check before leaving the station, the conductor politely asked "Is everyone on board?" It was a scene right out of John Ford's movie, *The Quiet Man.*

Tom and I then flew to London to see the sights there. I remember we decided to stay at a bed & breakfast, and the woman refused to believe that we were brother and sister. She wanted to rent us two separate rooms, but we insisted we needed one room with two beds. She thought we were an unmarried couple. We were able to persuade her when she saw our passports with the same name.

We traveled to Germany on the railroad in a third class compartment. The difference in fare between third class and first class was minimal. I remember asking my brother, "You must be crazy! Why did you buy third class tickets?" Our compartment was crowded with people carrying baskets full of strange smelling foods, and even one woman who was travelling, for some reason, with a live chicken (this was a new twist on "chicken in the basket").

Besides the characters in the third class compartment, I remember being awakened by a very brusque German policeman when we arrived at the German border. I had been sleeping and probably dreaming about the Nazis when the doors to the compartment flew open. My eyes popped open, and standing in the doorway was this man, in a long black leather raincoat, who looked to me like an SS captain, yelling "Achtung, Achtung." I was terrified. Of course, he was just checking passports, but that's the way the Germans did it in those days.

After spending some days in Germany, I decided to go to Paris. I figured I might never get there again. I had studied French for three years and I wanted to test it out. My brother was a little nervous about this, but I convinced him it was a good idea. I travelled by train to Paris, but this time I went first class. I think it was quite adventuresome of me to do this. As it turned out I met the sister of a friend of mine on a street in Paris. We were so glad to see one another. She was there with three girls who never wanted to leave their hotel room. We made a date to take the nightclub tour of Paris that evening.

In the meantime, I went strolling around Paris looking for a pair of Parisian shoes. I was determined to have a pair of Parisian shoes. While I was looking in a shop window, a man approached me and asked me what time it was. I said in French, I didn't understand him; I only spoke English. He immediately said he could speak English. He said he would help me purchase the shoes. So into the shop I went with this man; he was about 30 I would say.

He then invited me to a sidewalk café for a cup of coffee. I didn't see any harm in that, and we were sitting on the sidewalk so what could happen to me? As we sat there watching the crowds go by, he began to kiss my hand, then my wrist and then my arm. He asked me to go with him for the weekend to Madrid. I was shocked and said "What will I tell my mother?" He jumped up from his chair and was very aggravated and said, "That's the trouble with you American girls. You are always wondering what you will tell your mother."

Needless to say, I got rid of him. I went to the lobby of the hotel where my friend was staying and rang her room. Sure enough, her friends who never left their Paris hotel room were there and they invited me up.

That evening I was going out on the tour of Paris with my friend so I went back to my hotel to get ready. The way the tour worked was you booked the tour with the bell captain in your hotel, and at a certain time, a tour bus (a small one carrying about twelve passengers) picked you up in the lobby. So it was quite safe. Getting on the tour bus with me were three men from India. They had British accents and appeared to be gentlemen. Anyway, we picked up my friend and proceeded on the night club tour. We saw Paris by night, and it was a great experience. One of the stops on the tour was the Follies Bergère. We were shocked to see nude showgirls flying on swings through the air. My friend and I had led a sheltered life in Brooklyn. After we dropped my friend off at her hotel, the bus carrying me and the three Indian gentlemen proceeded to my hotel. Now I was a little nervous. The three men got in the lift with me, and they got off at the same floor as I did. I thought "this is not good" and proceeded toward my room, and they walked right along with me. I was thinking of screaming, but when they got to my door, they said they would wait until I was safely inside, as they wanted to be sure nothing happened to me. I never left the room again until morning even though the bathroom was down the hall. I had had enough adventure for one evening.

My trip to Europe was about ten years after World War II, and I saw many bombed out buildings and many men who were missing limbs. It was a sobering experience, and I was fortunate to have that experience so young. It gave me a graphic lesson of the consequences of the war that I had lived through as a child, but which had never directly touched me.

When I returned from Europe, my friend, Kathleen Gibbons, asked if I would go again with her, and I said yes, as there was much more to see. So we began to save our money for the next big trip.

My friends and I knew what we wanted in life and that was to have a home, husband and family, but before we did that, we wanted to have fun. So for the time between our 18th birthday and the day we got married, we were pretty frivolous, carefree girls bouncing around to all the dances in Brooklyn. In the 1950s in Brooklyn, every weekend there were these great dances at which you could meet tons of single Catholic young men. Naturally, we, as Catholics, only wanted to meet Catholic young men. It was the way we were raised, and our parents did not want us to date anyone who was not a Catholic. It made life much simpler, and our parents knew that. So these dances were usually held in parish halls. A parish hall is a meeting place which is part of the church building. It is used for social events. Every Catholic in Brooklyn was identified by the parish in which he or she lived. When a person was introduced to another person, invariably the first question asked was, "What Parish do you live in?" The answer to that question told you several things: whether the person was a Catholic, where he or she lived, and who you might know who would know the person. In other words, it was a way of checking whether the person was honorable or not. In those days, the boys had a saying that they would use to describe a girl they had met who lived too far away from them. No one had a car at that time so a boy from the Bronx would not date a girl from Brooklyn because she would be "geographically undesirable." That meant it was too far to travel on the subway to pursue the relationship. Of course, there were always exceptions to the rule. "Geographically undesirable" did not deter my Uncle Chris from pursuing my Aunt Peggy.

The great part about Brooklyn, and these dances, is that we all could dance like crazy. We went dancing on Friday, Saturday and Sunday, and then we went to work on Monday morning. I was a great dancer and so I always had a partner. Everyone wanted to dance with a great dancer and I spent so much time dancing that I got better and better.

As a matter of fact, when my fourth son was married, someone asked me and my husband how we could dance like that and how I knew where he was leading me. I told him that I had a "Masters in Dancing" and if he had danced his youth as frivolously away as we did, he would be a great dancer too, instead of a great cardiologist. My son's wedding took place the day before our 40th wedding anniversary so at midnight the orchestra played "As Time Goes By" and Jim and I got up to dance a special dance by ourselves. Afterwards, an old friend came up to us and said, "That was one of the most moving things I have ever seen at a wedding."

In Brooklyn, dancing was a way of life. We went dancing sometimes with a beau, but most times without, because there was always the possibility of meeting "Mr. Right." I met a lot of great dancers, but never "Mr. Right." As a matter of fact, one of my friends did meet her husband at one of these dances, and she is still married to him 44 years later. In those days in Brooklyn, girls were able to walk home alone late at night and never be attacked. Many times, my friends and I would be returning from a dance at one in the morning, and we would take a taxi to each house. When the last girl was left in the taxi, we would warn the taxi driver that we were taking down his number and that if our friend didn't arrive home within the next 1/2 hour, we would call the police and report him. Needless to say, taxi drivers made sure we all got safely to our door.

At that time, we had seven girls in our crowd. We usually went everywhere together, and we were known to boyfriends as "The Sneaker Debs." How we got that name I don't know, but it stuck to us for years.

Sneaker Debs at the beach: Anne White, Marie McCarthy, Theresa Donahue, Betty Keane and me

It Only Happens Now and Then …

We all dressed the same. Some days we wore Bermuda shorts and sneakers which no one else in Brooklyn wore so that set us apart. Whenever we were going out, we always called each other to see what the dress code was for the evening. To this day, we still call one another to find out what the other is wearing. My husband thinks this is crazy.

Because we travelled in this crowd of girls, we didn't meet a lot of guys who were interested in us because there were so many of us. One of the girls was beautiful, and she would dance all night with great looking guys, but when it came time to leave and go home, she would dance with anyone who had a car. She would get a ride home, and then she would tell the guy that her friends had to go with her. And so this poor guy got stuck driving seven girls home.

One night we were getting a ride from Manhattan to Brooklyn with a guy she had just met. Unfortunately, he had had a lot to drink. None of the girls drove then except me, and I realized immediately when I got in the car that this guy was drunk and was going to get us all killed. As we were driving over the Manhattan Bridge in the passing lane, I screamed, "We are going to be killed, we have to get out of here." When we got to the Brooklyn side of the Bridge, he stopped the car and threw us out. All my friends were furious with me, but I think I saved their lives. There we were in a very bad section of Brooklyn, with no transportation, so we stopped in a seedy bar (that's all there was around there), and I called my father, and he got out of his bed and drove down to pick us up. He wasn't too happy, but he did it.

There weren't too many girls in Brooklyn in 1954 who could drive a car, but I was one who could. My Dad taught me to drive when I was sixteen. We had a house in the "country" in upstate New York, and we went there every weekend, and it was up there that my Dad taught me to drive. When I was eighteen, I got a driver's license in Brooklyn. This was not easy because to get the license, you had to drive on the busy Brooklyn streets in all the traffic. Very few people passed the test the first time. As a matter of fact, my brother Tom who was an excellent driver failed the first time so no one thought I would pass, but I did. I remember it vividly because it was Christmas Eve when I took the test, and I left my office where a Christmas party was going on, to go with my Dad to take this test. When we got there, my Dad couldn't find the insurance papers for the car, and so it looked like they wouldn't let me take the test. I was angry with my Dad and told him so while the driving inspector was standing right there. Fortunately, my Dad did find the papers, and I jumped in the car with the inspector to take the test. I whizzed through the test because I was so angry, and all the while the inspector was lecturing me on showing proper respect for my father. Even after I had absolutely no difficulty parallel parking the car (this was the hardest thing for most people to do on a city street), I still figured this guy was so annoyed with me for being a spoiled brat that he was never going to pass me. I pulled the car out of the space in a fit of temper, and tapped the parked car in front of me. Usually, hitting a car was the "kiss of death" as far as the driver's license goes … I thought, "That's it."

In those days the test results came in the mail. My Dad said, "You failed." My brother Tom said, "You failed." So it was a great surprise to me when the driver's license came in the mail. I think I just breezed through the test in a fit of anger, and the inspector was so busy lecturing me on my bad manners, that he just passed me. Or maybe it was Christmas Eve, and he was in a good mood. My mother always said I was the best driver in the house and she would drive with me anywhere.

Getting a driver's license was a great thrill. My Dad was so good to me; he let me drive his new car if I was going someplace special. Shortly after getting the license, I drove with about four friends to see Washington, D.C. It was the first time I was down south, and it was a great adventure. We saw all the sights. We were all riding in this brand new Plymouth ... the car with the big fins. We went to Arlington Cemetery one day, very close to closing. We were visiting the Tomb of the Unknown Soldier and we were kidding around with the Honor Guard. They asked us if we wanted to guard the Unknown Soldier, and I said yes. So one of the guards gave me his rifle and I marched before the monument with his rifle on my shoulder. It was probably the most daring thing I had ever done, as I was a stickler for going by the rules. I can't believe I did that, but it is true.

The next trip we took was for a week to Cape Cod. We had rented a house thinking we might meet some nice young men. This house was located near a body of water, and one night we were out in a terrible thunderstorm. When we got home to the house the road was flooded, and I remember thinking "what will happen to my father's new car." I refused to drive down the road to the house, and told the girls to get out of the car. They carried on that they would get all wet, their dresses would be ruined, etc., but I was adamant. The car was not going any further. I found a piece of high ground and parked the car up on it, and told the girls to get out. They couldn't believe I would do that to them. Anyway, they all took off their dresses, and it was a sight to see. In the thunder and lightning, you could see five girls running down the road in their slips. In those days, we always wore slips. The next day when we woke up, there was water all over, but the car was on dry ground. We waited a few hours and the water subsided, and we got back to the car, started it up and proceeded to our next adventure on Cape Cod. By the way, we never met anyone who was interested in us on that trip.

Being able to access "wheels" opened up a new horizon for the Sneaker Debs. As the years went on, some of the other girls got driver's licenses as well. Marie Boyle, a dear friend of mine, had a license, but didn't have much experience driving. One weekend, she asked her father if we could use his car to go to the Jersey Shore, where, once again, in search of a husband, we had rented a house for the summer. Five of us were in the car going to the shore, and this was before air conditioned cars, or at least this car didn't have air-conditioning. We were in the Lincoln Tunnel, and Marie was nervously driving the car. I was in the front seat as the only other driver in the car. The car kept swerving back and forth across the yellow line in the tunnel, and I kept screaming at Marie to "get a grip on it" and "drive the car straight." She was having a nervous breakdown. In the meantime, Betty and Marie Mac were giggling in the back and our friend, Peg, was reading "War and Peace." When we finally emerged from the tunnel, a man was screaming at us and pointing to our back tire. We finally figured out that we had a flat tire, and that was why Marie couldn't drive the car straight. We pulled to the side and some nice young man changed our tire. Those were the days when men changed ladies' tires. After this experience, Marie decided she could no longer drive the car, so I took over. It seems to me that I was always "taking over." For some reason, I was always organizing outings, paying the bill, figuring out the tip, and so forth. This was probably because I was now a secretary, but I seem to remember doing this all the while I was hanging around with these girls. I can even remember figuring out the bill at the soda shop and collecting the money.

Continuing with the story of this weekend at the shore, it went from bad to worse. When we finally arrived at Manasquan, where we had rented the house for the summer, we stopped at the grocery store to stock up on supplies. Marie was now holding the keys to the car because, after all, it was her father's car. When we came out of the grocery store with the bags of groceries, for some reason, after Marie opened the trunk of the car to store the groceries, she put the keys on the hood of the car behind us. We were so busy talking, which was something we did constantly, that we didn't notice the car backing up and pulling away with the keys.

And then there we were with no keys. Along came a boyfriend of Betty's and he solved the dilemma by teaching me, of course, how to hotwire the car. I stuck my head under the hood and put these two wires together and the car started.

That evening when we were about to go out, I gathered all my friends around and told them to pick one place and that was where we were going to stay for the night. Usually, when we went out, if we didn't like a place, meaning we didn't like the fellows in the place, we left and went somewhere else. We were constantly moving from place to place on a Saturday night at the shore. But this

Saturday, I told them it would be different because I was not keen to hotwire the car in my beautiful white dress. One hotwire was all we were getting … period. So we decided on the Allaire which was the best place in Spring Lake for meeting single people. We were all sitting down with some guys, and the guy next to me began to get fresh, so I stood up and hit him on the head with my evening bag which just happened to have about 25 silver dollars in it and was quite heavy. After he got this whack on the head, and slid under the table, I said to the girls "Get up, we're leaving." They said, "But, Fitzi, you said we couldn't leave." I proceeded to walk to the door and they all followed me as people tried to revive the guy who was under the table. And so there we were outside hotwiring the car again.

I should explain here how I came to have $25 worth of silver dollars in my evening bag. On the Friday that we were leaving for the Shore, I went home expecting to find my parents there. But they had already left for their weekend in the country. This was bad because I was intending to borrow some money from my Dad for the trip. In those days, there was no ATM machine, and my Dad was really my banker. Whenever I needed money, I went to him. Now I was in a dilemma. Then I remembered my Dad's stash of silver dollars. I took 25 of them, put them in my pocketbook and off I went to the Shore. It was just a loan, and I always paid him back when I got paid. My Dad always had money in the house … for emergencies … and I considered my trip to Manasquan an emergency.

I remember that weekends at the Jersey Shore were frivolous and fun, but we never lost sight of the fact that we were to go to Mass on Sunday morning no matter how late we were out the night before. On one particular weekend, we arrived home so late that all the girls laid down on their beds in their dresses, hose, earrings, makeup, etc., and slept briefly until it was time to go to Sunday Mass. We just slept on top of the covers so that we wouldn't be wrinkled going to church. No one ever went to church in "casual dress."

I didn't go to the shore as much as my friends because my parents had a house in the "country" and my mother liked me to drive them there on the weekends. So every other weekend, I went to the country. I liked the country as I had my own room there, and I always brought a lot of books and I would sit on the porch, listen to the crickets and read.

After years of vacations in the Catskills, my Mom and Dad had purchased their own house in the country around 1954 when I was eighteen and had finished high school. My father and mother always wanted to get out of the city for the hot summers, and an opportunity arose to buy a house on two acres in the Shawangunk Mountains about 90 miles from the city. They both agreed that living in the mountains in the summer would be a great respite from hot Brooklyn. I think they also wanted to give my brother, Joseph, and me, something to do besides hanging around in the city. I wasn't wild about going to such a quiet place for the weekends in the summer, but I knew my parents wanted me to go, so we compromised and one weekend I would go to the shore with friends and one weekend to the country house near New Paltz. I never regretted doing that, and we had some great times there. Often during the weekends we visited back and forth with my Uncle Chris and his family at their less rustic country house in the village of Rhinebeck, New York, on the Hudson River.

One thing I remember about the country house was that my Mother and Father loved it, and that was the most important thing. They really longed for the green hills of Ireland, and this was as close as they could get to it while living in Brooklyn. It was a quiet, tranquil place and after a hot steamy week working in the city, it was a refreshing change of pace for them.

Over the years I spent a lot of happy times at this house. We had this great lake near us where we went swimming. It was called Lake Minnewaska, and it was quite beautiful. It was a pure azure blue mountain lake, and because it had a high acidity level and little algae, there were no fish and the water was fresh and aqua colored. In my mind I envisioned Indians canoeing across the Lake. We often went canoeing and hiking up there, and my parents enjoyed being there and close to nature.

At Lake Minnewaska, there was a wonderful Victorian era hotel, and we would go there for dinner on special occasions like Mother's Day and Father's Day. It was like stepping back in time. I appreciated Lake Minnewaska much more once I was married and had children. More on that later …

I remember how we would go to the country house in the fall. One time we went there … it was my brother Tom, his fiancée Rosemary, my mother and me. My mother loved to make a fire in the stove in the dining room and bake an apple pie … it was always delicious in the cool mountain air. This particular time, while she was making the pie, Tom, Rosemary and I went on a hike. It was supposed to be a short walk up the mountain behind the house, but my brother kept going and going. Rosemary and I were not properly dressed or shod for a long trek in the woods, but we gamely followed, and then the dark came in upon us quickly and we were lost. I was amazed that my brother could get lost because he was always so confident with a compass. In the dark, without his trusty compass and without a match or flashlight, he was not prepared for a cold autumn evening in the woods with two hysterical girls. We were trekking around on dangerous cliffs and we could have fallen through a crevice and gotten killed. We wandered on and on and finally, we saw the headlights from cars on a highway. When we eventually bushwhacked our way out of the forest to the road, many miles from our house, we were exhausted. My mother was sure that we were dead, and she was under great stress especially since Rosemary was just visiting and not one of the family yet.

It took us a couple of hours to reach the house, and there was nothing my mother could do during this time as we did not have a phone. When we finally arrived, my mother said, "Forget about the dinner and the pie, we are going home." It was the first time I had ever seen my mother so upset. I think it was because there was no way she could help us and she just had to sit there and wait for our return. There was nowhere for her to go to get help as she couldn't drive the car. When the sun went down in the country, we never ventured far from the house because the woods were so dark. For us to be lost in this darkness was very hard on my mother. Years later, she told me the major regret of her life was that she never learned to drive. I actually tried to teach her once, but by that time she was in her sixties, and we decided it was too late to learn. She would have made a great driver because she was totally skilled at riding a bicycle, and she was very mechanical, but she said there are certain things you should learn young and driving was one of them. That is probably why she encouraged me to drive when I was just sixteen.

Reminiscing about my brother Tom, and his fiancée, Rosemary, brings to mind the story of their wedding.

Tom met Rosemary on a blind date while he was at Fordham University and Rosemary was at Mount St. Vincent College. When Tom graduated, they had an understanding, and after he served his two years in the Army (he was drafted during the Korean War), he returned home and he and Rosemary were married in Westfield, New Jersey. The wedding was held in February near Valentine's Day and it was snowing that morning as we drove from Brooklyn to Westfield. We had never been to Westfield before and my Dad was driving the car, and my mother was her usual nervous wreck when my Dad drove. So in a blinding snowstorm, we drove about two hours from our home to this wedding.

What I really remember about the wedding was the reception. It was held in the Westfield Woman's Club, which was very posh, and they served a delicious buffet luncheon of hot chicken salad, and waiters were walking around with trays of champagne. Coming from Brooklyn, we actually had never been to a reception where only champagne was served, and it was very impressive. When the reception was over, Tom and Rosemary left on their honeymoon, and Rosemary's uncle, Jim Vanick, invited all the guests back to his home for drinks. About 100 people descended on the Vanicks' beautiful big Tudor house. To us, coming from Brooklyn, it looked like a mansion, and I think maybe it was. The most interesting thing at the house was the way Mrs. Vanick had all the gifts displayed on a long table on the sun porch. It was like something you would see in a Katherine Hepburn movie. Every gift was labeled somehow so that you could see who gave the gift. I was very impressed. They also had a man on the porch "watching the gifts" so that no one could take them. I don't think they thought we would take the gifts, but they did not want to go to the wedding and leave the house and all the gifts unattended. I had never seen anything like that before, nor have I since.

Besides going to the shore in the summer, we Sneaker Debs amused ourselves in the winter by doing things in the city. Since Betty and I worked in the city, we often went ice skating in Central Park. An ice skating rink had just been built there, and it was very convenient for us. We would leave our skates in our desks and at least one night a week we would go ice skating. Central Park was perfectly safe then; no one gave a thought to the possibility of crime. Some of the girls who were school teachers would travel all the way from Brooklyn to Central Park to skate with us.

Betty Keane had this great boyfriend, Roy Guidi (I think he was the first one to call us the Sneaker Debs), and he had been a hockey player in college. He was the nicest guy. He would take each girl on a turn around the rink, and having Roy guide us around was terrific. Because he was holding us up, all of a sudden, we felt like an ice queen.

Actually, all the girls were pretty good skaters, but I wasn't. I didn't understand this because I could roller skate fine. My left ankle kept turning in, and I couldn't stand straight on the blades. One night, Betty used my skates and she couldn't skate either; her left ankle kept turning in. Roy decided to look at the blade, and sure enough, the blade was crooked on the boot. We took the skates to a skate shop and the man moved the blade to the correct place, and voila, I could skate like everyone else. So if your ankles are turning in when you skate, have the blades checked.

While having lunch with some old friends recently, we were reminiscing about our madcap days going out in the city. We recalled one story where we all went to 86th street to go to an Irish dance. This was a very ethnic section of the city, mostly German and Irish, and we went there to meet Irish guys who could dance. Before going to the "Tuxedo Ballroom" where the dance was held, we all stopped at a German brauhaus to kill some time. It was called the Lorelei. We checked our coats, and for some reason, once again, I was holding all the coat checks. We sat down, ordered a beer, and then realized there was a $5.00 cover charge. That meant that to just sit down, you had to pay $5.00 in addition to the beer. We were horrified, as we didn't have enough money for this place and the dance, so we hatched a plan to escape without paying the bill. We were going to leave the table two at a time by pretending to go to the powder room. The only problem was we had to get our coats, and I was holding all the coat checks. I gave each girl a coat check and told her to just take the coat she received even if it wasn't hers, put in on, and quickly walk out. Now it happened that Betty had a beautiful red coat with a grey Persian fur collar which was brand new. When she got to the coat check room, they handed her a long black coat which of course didn't fit her. She was just about to say it wasn't her coat when she remembered what I had said. When the last two of us went to the coat check room, my friend, Marie, got Betty's beautiful red coat.

Unfortunately, Marie was really tall, and she tried to squeeze into this little coat. By now, the hat check girl was beginning to get suspicious. Marie and I ran out the door, and the waiter was running after us waving his dish towel and saying, "Stop, you didn't pay the bill." But we escaped.

Speaking of escapes reminds me of another tale with the infamous Marie McCarthy. Marie was always either coming or going to some place. She never stood still. On one of these occasions she persuaded me to go to Columbia University to a tea dance. This was a dance held in the afternoon. It was really a mixer where young men and women met. To do this, we had to take the train to 116th Street in Manhattan. This was a long way from Brooklyn. As it turned out, we missed our stop and got off the train in the middle of Harlem, and when we came out of the subway, we were the only two white people on the street. Marie was a tall, willowy girl with a mass of blond hair. She was quite an attraction. Everyone was staring at her, and we got so nervous, we raced across the street, and ran down the subway stairs with people actually running after us. When we approached the escalator to go down to the subway platform, we were running so fast we didn't realize that we were running down the up escalator. When we got to the bottom, we decided to return to Brooklyn, as we thought it was safer there and our days of venturing into the northern reaches of Manhattan were over.

It is hard to believe in this day and age when eating out is so commonplace that eating out in Brooklyn when I was a girl was a rare occasion. In the 1940s and 1950s very few people went out to eat. It just wasn't done. My family always ate at home, so it came as a great surprise to me and my brothers when one day in May, my father announced that we were going out to dinner on Sunday. We were all shocked as we had never actually been to a restaurant as a family. But that particular Sunday was Mother's Day, and my father was really getting into the American culture. My mother was concerned that it would be too expensive to take the whole family out, but my father had made up his mind. After the 12 o'clock Mass, we all got into the family car and drove to the Hamilton House restaurant in Bay Ridge, Brooklyn. This was a beautiful restaurant, and I really don't know how my father even heard about it. We all had a wonderful time, and it was a great experience. I never forgot it. I believe my mother was very happy that my father had thought about doing this for her on that occasion.

On another Mother's Day, when Jim and I were dating, my dad took us to the hotel at Lake Minnewaska for Sunday dinner. This was quite an experience, as the hotel had an elegant dining room. It was a large Victorian style room with high ceilings and French doors that opened onto a wide veranda that went all around the hotel. There was no air conditioning in those days, but the breezes from the lake cooled the dining room.

The tables were covered with white linen and there were all sorts of waiters and bus boys flying around the room. It was quite a dining experience. After dinner the guests would go out on the veranda and relax in wonderful wicker rocking chairs. It gave me the feeling of being on the deck of a great ocean liner. Years later, the hotel was completely destroyed by a fire that marked the end of an era never to be seen again.

At my first job, I had another eating out experience that I have never forgotten. The girls in my office had a habit of eating out on "pay day." So, on my first pay day, I joined a couple of the girls for dinner at a restaurant in the city. After we were eating awhile, one of the girls remarked on the strange way I held my knife and fork. I was really taken aback. I never suspected there was any problem with my table manners. Nothing more was said about it, but I was quite chagrined. When I returned home, I told my mother what had happened, but she assured me that I was eating properly.

We figured out that because we were Irish and all our friends and relatives were Irish, we were eating European style. As is the custom in Europe, we held our fork in our left hand while cutting and eating. In America, food is cut the same way, but the fork is transferred from the left hand to the right hand before eating.

I was certainly relieved to hear this. The next day when I went to work I told the girls that "I ate in the European manner just like the King and Queen of England." That settled that, but I decided as long as I was an American, I would now eat like an American.

An interesting anecdote related to this story is that one day I was watching a spy movie set during World War II in which an American spy was sitting in a café somewhere in Germany, and he was being watched by the Gestapo (the movie was *OSS* with Alan Ladd). He was a perfect spy and had all the European mannerisms, except he made one fatal error. While dining in the café, he picked up his knife and fork and proceeded to eat in the American style. The Gestapo knew at once that he was an American spy. I never forgot that scene. It reminded me of me.

Another eating out experience I can recall involved my brother Tom. There was a very popular diner in Brooklyn at this time called Toomey's. I had never been there and always wanted to go. When I was about twenty-one, my parents went to Ireland for a twenty-fifth anniversary trip. My brother Tom and I were left to fend for ourselves, and one night I, who had never cooked anything, decided to make dinner for Tom. I intended to make a can of peas as part of the dinner. For some strange reason, I put the whole can, unopened, into a pot of cold water to boil. In a little while, the can exploded, and the peas flew all over the kitchen. Tom was aghast and said, "Put on your hat, Patsy, we're going to Toomey's." I replied, "Oh good, I'm going to Toomey's!" Tom remarked on the way to the diner that my culinary skills could use some improvement, but I took no notice. As my mother would have said, "It is an ill wind that blows no good."

When I think about eating out in the Forties and Fifties, I have to mention that we actually had "take-out." In those days, take-out food was sold in German or Jewish delicatessens which were always owned by European immigrants. Many times on Sundays, when we were returning from our outings in Prospect Park, my Dad would stop at "Ben & Sol's Deli" and buy something for supper. We never ate in the deli; we always took the food home. Usually, my Dad would buy two absolutely delicious overstuffed corned beef sandwiches and six extra pieces of rye bread. He did this because the two sandwiches actually contained enough corned beef to make five generous sandwiches. My mother said, "It is like the miracle of the loaves and fishes." If you ordered the sandwiches with mustard, they would take a square out of waxed paper and pour the most yummy mustard onto it and form the paper into a tube, similar to what a person would use to decorate a cake, and then you could squeeze the mustard onto your sandwich when you got home. I personally think that Jewish corned beef is far superior to Irish corned beef, St. Patrick's Day notwithstanding!

Another great treat I can vividly remember from Ben & Sol's was their delicious all beef frankfurters with mustard and sauerkraut. These were cooked on a grill in their front window to entice you in. I can still recall, as if it were today, the wonderful aroma of the franks my mother treated us to on our way home from LaGuardia Airport after seeing my father off on his trip to Ireland in 1947.

It Only Happens Now and Then …

My Mother, Nellie Carey

Now I come to my mother who had a great influence on my life. I have told you some stories of my mother when she was young and how she married my father. Now I will write some remembrances of her.

My mother always told me that there was nothing I couldn't do if I wanted to do it. That thought stuck with me through my whole life. I always approached every problem with the attitude that if someone else could do it, I could do it. She instilled in me a great sense of confidence. My friends used to say that they thought my father must have loved me very much because I was such an outgoing and friendly person. I guess the gregarious part of me came from my father, but the practical side of me came from my mother. She was a no nonsense woman with a great brain. Although she was only educated through the 8th grade, she could read and spell to an extraordinary degree and was an avid doer of crossword puzzles.

She was apprenticed when she was about twelve to a dressmaker in Waterford, Ireland, and there she learned her skills as a dressmaker. Her whole family was of an engineering bent, and I believe she had that too. She could fix anything in the house; she could wallpaper and paint and repair bicycles. Nothing seemed to be a problem to her if she wanted to do it. I guess that's where she got the idea that I was the same, and that I could do anything if I wanted to.

First of all, I want to say that I never thanked her for all the great things she did for me. I hope that she knew that I appreciated her, but one should always thank their mother for the countless things they do for us. I never realized how difficult being a mother was until I became a mother myself. One never can appreciate one's mother until one has had to deal with children. As I look back on it, I marvel at the work that was done by women like my mother. She had to do all the diapers for the children, had to prepare the food, as there was no prepared food, had to sterilize the dishes, and had to stay up all night sometimes taking care of sick babies. My Dad never took care of any kind of babies, sick or otherwise. She had to walk us to school every morning when we were little, and that included getting us up, feeding us a good breakfast, and getting my younger brother Joseph, bundled up and into his carriage to walk to school. (We walked back ourselves.)

She did her shopping every day … there were no supermarkets before the war … and prepared, as I recall, a hot supper every evening. In the meantime, she washed our clothes using a washing board, as we had no washing machine. She hung them out to dry on the line, and she ironed all the clothes. On weekends, she entertained Irish friends with Sunday dinners or Saturday night suppers. Then on Monday she started again on her routine. Part of that routine, of course, was climbing up three flights of stairs with the groceries and the baby. Her routine also consisted of getting the children out every day for an airing. Every morning mothers in Brooklyn were out by 10 a.m. walking their babies.

In addition to all of the above chores, she made all of her clothes and all of my clothes. She never sewed for my brothers, as she was interested in fashion, and boy's clothes were not fashionable.

My mother, Ellen Fitzgerald

It Only Happens Now and Then ...

When I was a girl, especially when I was in high school, I was the best dressed girl in school. Every Monday I had a new outfit. Sewing was my mother's hobby, and every week she would buy fabric, usually a remnant, which is a piece, or maybe two pieces, of left-over fabric from some bolt of cloth that was discontinued. From this she would piece the fabric together, depending on the design which was on the fabric, and make some kind of an outfit for me. Sometimes, it was a skirt; sometimes, it was a dress, and sometimes, it was a jacket or a coat. She looked at the pieces of fabric as an engineering project, and she would cut it out very cleverly so that all the stripes, flowers, etc., matched. She was a genius the way she could do this. My brothers and I would watch her sewing for hours. Of course, she only did this in the day when my Dad wasn't around. He could not stand the house in disarray so before he came home from work my mother would pick up all the pieces, pattern, pins and ironing board and put them away. This was very frustrating to a creative person, and so years later, when I moved out of the house, my mother changed my bedroom into a sewing room, and she blissfully walked out of the chaos and shut the door on the piles of fabric and pins that lay around the room. My Dad didn't mind this because he couldn't see it.

I want to mention that everyone in my family always wears shoes, and this is the result of my mother's sewing. For surely, you would get a pin in your foot if you walked around the house in bare feet. One time my brother Tom was standing too close to the sewing machine and the needle went through his finger nail ... ugh. Fortunately, it didn't kill him, but my mother almost did. One of the things my mother could not abide was disobedient children. I am sure she blamed Tom for being too near the sewing machine.

She was a very strict woman. She knew that it was not easy in Brooklyn to raise children. She was always telling my brothers that she didn't want their name on the "blotter." That meant that she didn't want to have to go to the police station if they got in any trouble. She warned them to stay out of trouble, or she "would kill them." Of course, that is no longer a sanctioned childrearing approach, but in those days, it worked. Neither of my brothers was ever in the police station, thank God.

My mother was determined that my two brothers would go to college. There would be no debating about this in our family. Of course, she wasn't concerned that I go to college. I think in those days girls were just supposed to get married, and that it was considered a waste of money to educate a girl. Anyway, when we children were young, my Grandfather Fitzgerald died, and so my father could have finally inherited Knockhouse. My mother told me that when the news came, they sat down and thought what was best for them and their children. I think my Dad would have returned to Ireland, but my mother thought the educational opportunities for her children were in America. So, they decided to give up the inheritance and stay here. I don't believe they ever regretted their decision.

My parents moved to Bedford Avenue, because they wanted to live in a place near a great Jesuit prep school for my brothers and a great high school for me. I believe my mother instigated this move. Both of these schools were within a short walk of our house. The next problem was getting into these schools. They were hard to get in and hard to stay in, especially Brooklyn Prep where my brothers eventually went. My mother had made up her mind that this was where they would go, and she told them she expected them to get in. She never considered any other school for them. I think she put the "fear of God" into them, and they didn't want to think about the consequences of not getting in this school, so they did.

My brother, Tom, who is a very smart guy, like his mother's side, went to Brooklyn Prep on a half scholarship. My Dad paid for half, and it was expensive, and the other half of the tuition was paid by my brother who did some work in the church, and also was an altar boy and served funerals, weddings, etc. He didn't mind being pulled out of class to serve funerals, as he was not a scholar even though he had a great brain. He just didn't like to study, and he didn't need to study too hard, as he always managed to pass ... just about.

The passing grade in Prep was 70. If you didn't get that, they threw you out. Needless to say, Tom did not want to deal with my mother if he got thrown out, so he always managed to stay in. My brother Joseph was another story. He was a scholar and took Latin and Greek at the same time. He was on a half-scholarship also. One day when they called for him to go to church to serve a funeral, he refused, as he was in the middle of a complicated Greek lesson.

Of course, my parents were called over to discuss the fact that he would not leave the class to serve the funeral Mass. Right there, my mother, without consulting my father, said to the priest that they were giving up the scholarship and from then on would pay full tuition. My father wasn't too happy with that, but my mother was adamant. If she had a real scholar on her hands, she was not going to deny him the education that he deserved. It was a great sacrifice for my parents to do this while they were paying college tuition for Tom, but they managed. They never regretted it. They were very proud of their sons, and they were proud of the fact that they had put them both through college, and lived to see them graduate.

You will notice that my parents were not concerned with educating me, their daughter. That's because my father believed that I would get married and when I did I would stop working. He believed that women would be happier if they had a husband, home and children, and as I look back on it, I think he was right. Of course, that was in the 1950s, and times have changed. Now people need to be educated so that they can make a livelihood if their circumstances change through divorce, etc.

My mother was a woman of many talents. It seemed to me she literally could do anything with her hands. She could paint, wallpaper, fix bicycle tires, make repairs in our house, knit, crochet, embroider, but mostly she could sew. And if anyone would remember anything about her it was the fact that she loved to sew. Of course, I was the beneficiary of all her sewing. She said I had a great figure, and she loved to make clothes for me because they looked good on me. She was like an artist who created an outfit and wanted it to be properly displayed. She made her own clothes also, but I always remember that she had many dresses that were unfinished because she was a little heavy, and she just wasn't happy with the way the dresses fit her. I imagine it's very difficult to make one's own clothes because it's difficult to fit them. I do remember when I was a very little girl that my mother had a "dummy form" and that is what she fitted her dresses on. I guess it was made for her size when she was slim, and then when she got heavy, it wasn't any good any more. Anyway, she made all my clothes, dresses, coats, suits, and skirts, until the day I got married. I never wore store bought clothes. I had the most beautiful wardrobe in Brooklyn, and all I had to do was buy the accessories to go with the outfits.

Every day I left my house dressed like a fashion plate, thanks to my mother. I remember one time I was going to the Fordham University prom, and she made me the most gorgeous white tulle gown with sparkling butterflies all over it. It was a masterpiece.

I always assumed my mother would make my wedding dress, and all of her friends and my friends were waiting to see what she would design. When I asked her what she had in mind for my wedding gown, she said she had no intention of making the wedding gown. This came as a great shock to me. She was very superstitious, and she told me she would never make my wedding gown as it was hard luck for the bride or her mother to touch the wedding gown with a needle. She told me to go to Lord & Taylor and pick out a gown, and when I found one I liked, she would come and see it.

So my friend, Betty Keane, and I went to Lord & Taylor. The first gown I put on was the gown for me. I didn't have to look any further. I was amazed as I thought we would spend the whole day looking for this gown. Anyway, the gown fit perfectly, and my mother came to New York to see it. When I put it on, she called in the seamstress and proceeded to tell her what adjustments to make so that the gown was exactly perfect. This all was going to cost additional money and I didn't feel it was necessary, but my mother was adamant. She told the seamstress that my left shoulder was slightly lower than my right shoulder, and an adjustment should be made there, and that the left sleeve had to be shortened a quarter of an inch. I thought this was truly nuts, but my mother insisted on it being perfectly fitted. She had been making my clothes so long that she knew the imperfections in my body. Of course, there was no dissuading her, and the seamstress made the two adjustments, which by the way, cost $60.00 which in those days was a lot of money added to the price of the gown.

When I reflect on this now, I have to laugh as one of my mother's favorite savings was "A blind man would be glad to see it." Whenever anyone complained about anything being not right, she would immediately say, "A blind man would be glad to see it." But when it came to this wedding gown, nothing short of perfect would do. I have to say here that I have used this saying many times in my life in dealing with all sorts of situations.

My mother was so superstitious that the night before the wedding when I tried on my veil, and it needed a few stitches to keep it in place, she called my Aunt Peggy to come down and put the stitches in the veil. My poor Aunt Peggy was a nervous wreck as she couldn't sew and never had sewn anything in her life. My mother had Peggy thread the needle, and then proceeded to tell Aunt Peggy where to put the needle in and where to take it out. It was strange, but she would not touch the gown with the needle.

Many years later I met a woman who told me she had just finished making her daughter's wedding gown, and I was aghast, as I remembered what my mother had said when I got married. Two weeks before her daughter's wedding, this woman died suddenly.

Another time, I was at a shower for the daughter-in-law of a friend of mine, and the guests were discussing how the bride-to-be's mother made the gown. My mother's old superstition popped into my mind, and I thought "this is not good." The marriage lasted three months. I was beginning to think that there was something to this "old wives' tale." Needless to say, I have no daughters, but I would never touch my daughter's wedding gown with a needle.

I remember that my mother made me beautiful clothes (a real trousseau) for my wedding, and that she was sewing for weeks. She had made me a green dress for a "going away" outfit, and then about four days before the wedding, she told me she was not happy with the going away outfit because it was green and green was a hard luck color. She then went out and bought new material and whipped up a beige silk dress. She said it was more befitting a bride. She said she had no real objection to green clothes, but it was not suitable for the beginning of life's journey into marriage. As I said, she was very superstitious.

When I was expecting my first child, she sent me a trunk full of wonderful maternity clothes, including dresses for going out on special occasions, and a wonderful yellow woolen coat which became one of my favorite garments.

She was so good to me, and so generous of heart. I never told her how much I appreciated all the things she had done for me. She helped me raise my sons, and she was a major influence on them. She was a woman of great courage, and when she was dying of cancer, she never complained. Complaining was not in her nature. She was not a demonstrative woman, but I know she loved me because she was so generous to me.

She was very fond of my husband, Jim, and she told me once that I was so fortunate to have found such a "gentle man." She told me this one night after Jim had been up to her room to have a cup of tea with her. Near the end of her life, when she was too ill to come downstairs, Jim would go up to her room on the third floor every evening and talk to her about sports, especially the Mets. She was an avid baseball fan and she looked forward to these visits from my husband. It was after one of these visits that she told me what a gentleman Jim was.

My mother had a great sense of humor, and even though she was in great pain, she was able to see the humor in situations. For example, one summer day, I was looking out the window of my kitchen and I could see my mother dozing as she was sitting in her chair. I remember thinking that maybe she will pass away peacefully in that chair, but the next thing I saw was her jumping out of the chair and running to the back of the house. It seems that Jim, who was painting the back of the house, had reached out too far on the ladder and had fallen off. My mother was right there to help him, and then she rushed into the house to make him a cup of tea. A cup of tea was my mother's answer to life's most serious problems. But a cup of tea would not solve this problem, and Jim and I had to rush off to the emergency room because his arm was broken. Once again, my mother had to come to the rescue and take care of four little boys, make their dinner and get them ready for bed. When we came home hours later from the emergency room, and I apologized to my mother for burdening her with all this, she said, "I can't die yet; I don't think you and Jim are capable of taking care of these children without me." We all had another cup of tea and laughed about that, and to tell the truth, my mother actually lived for another year or so after that despite her advanced illness.

She was really a courageous woman. I recall a weekend trip with Jim, the four boys and my mother to her old country house in the Shawangunk Mountains above New Paltz. At this time in her life (she was about 76), she was very ill and very frail, but she wanted to go. We drove up there in my brother Joe's Cadillac which we were using because Joe and his family were in England and he had left the car with us for safekeeping. It was a huge car, and the seven of us fit in it with no problem ... of course, those were the days before seatbelts and car seats for kids. Jim and three boys were in the back and I was driving with my mother and young Jim in the front. My mother didn't like to drive with anyone but me. She had the utmost confidence in my driving skills and always said I was the best driver in the family. When we got to the country and unloaded the car, my mother went to lie down because she was exhausted from the trip.

Jim was sitting on the porch and he called me out to talk to him. He told me that he had injured his eye, and that we would have to return home so that he could get to an eye doctor. He thought his retina was detaching. This was a very serious situation because Jim only had vision in this eye. For a few minutes, we didn't know how to handle this, and then I went in to speak to my mother about it. She was lying on the bed and couldn't get up because the pain was so bad in her back. She told me to "pull her up," which I did, and then she told me that I should immediately drive back to Montclair with Jim. She said she would take care of two of the boys and I should take the other two home.

It was amazing how she just stood up and took charge of
a very serious situation. She said she would be all right
and she would not let anything happen, meaning she
would just not die right there. You have to remember
there was no telephone in the house, no way to reach us if
anything happened. But she was so determined that I was
sure that nothing would happen while she was in charge.
I drove home with Jim, young Jim and Mark and left
Phillip and Stephen with her. She took care of them for a
few days until I returned to bring everyone home. By that
time Jim was having an operation on his retina. I
remember that when we packed up the stuff for the
return trip, she said that was the last time she would ever
see the country house again. She wasn't sad, she was just
practical, and that was the way she was. She loved that
country house … she had so many happy memories there.

At this time, my mother became gravely ill. She died on
November 20th, 1977. It was a sad day for all of us and I
was especially concerned how my son Stephen would take
the news of her death. He had been away on a Boy Scout
overnight, and when he returned I told him the news. He
remembered that my mother's good friend had died the
week before, and so when I told him the news he said,
"Now she will be with her best friend in Heaven." I was
very moved by this. It was such a charming thing to say.

Before closing the chapter on my mother, I want to once
again stress what a woman of courage she was. When she
finally went to the hospital for the last time, the doctors
told her she had bone cancer. I went to see her, and she
said, "Patsy, I am going to die," and I said, "I know,
Mom. Just do it easy. Close your eyes and go to sleep."
And that's exactly what she did. We never spoke another
word again. She just closed her eyes and accepted God's

will. She wanted to go to heaven and not be a burden to anyone.

Here I want to add a few words about how kind Jim was to me throughout my mother's final illness. He was so thoughtful and caring. Every night when I would return home from my vigil at my mother's bedside, he would read me an uplifting poem to help calm me down and bring me peace. I will never forget his kindness.

People have asked me how and when my mother came to live with us. In 1975, when my mother was battling her second bout with breast cancer, she became very frail. She always knew there was a place for her in our home, but she never wanted to give up her independence. So she would travel back and forth to Brooklyn on the bus. She would usually come to Montclair on a Friday and return to Brooklyn either Monday or Tuesday. She began to stay longer and longer, and she would even stay a second weekend without returning to Brooklyn. One day I looked at her and I knew it was time for her to move to Montclair permanently. I simply said, "Mom, you are never going to Brooklyn again; you are going to stay here." It was as simple as that. I think she was greatly relieved that I made that decision for her.

I called my brothers and told them of the decision and asked them to move her things from Brooklyn to Montclair. They were happy to do so. My mother only wanted a few things from her apartment, as she was not a person who was obsessed with material possessions. She settled in permanently on our third floor, and the children were always happy to go up and visit "Grandma's house." It was as if she had lived with us always, and I think she was happy and comfortable and felt safe living with us.

It Only Happens Now and Then …

Courtship and Marriage

Now I am going to come to the part of my memoir that I know my ten granddaughters want to hear. They are always asking me how I met "grandpa" … so here it is. I met Jim in the summer of 1956 when I was 21.

I was working at that time as a secretary in the offices of the company that manufactured Martex towels; I was in the elevator going to the 5th floor where my office was; I was wearing a beautiful blue and white check dress and a blue roller hat (I always wore a hat), white gloves, etc., and into the elevator walked a very tall dark haired young man with glasses. I immediately recognized him as someone I had seen in grammar school many years ago, and I said, "I know you. Didn't you go to St. Francis of Assisi to grammar school?" He seemed to be somewhat taken aback by my statement, and before he could answer, he left the elevator at the 3rd floor. Later that evening when I was walking to the subway to go home, I met him again. He was talking to someone I knew who properly introduced us. Once again, I said, "I know you from St. Francis of Assisi. We went to the same grammar school." It seems I recognized him, but he didn't know me at all. I told him that he hadn't changed in all those years and what I distinctly remembered about him was his glasses. Anyway, one word led to another and the next thing we knew we were both going down the stairs into the subway, and we were both riding on the same train home to Brooklyn. This was the beginning of a subway adventure that was to last for about five years.

Jim was in the elevator that day because he was applying for a job, which he got, in the cost accounting department. In the early days of our friendship, because we lived not too far from each other we traveled on the same train every day. Sometimes we met and sometimes we didn't. One day Jim invited me out on a double date. A double date is when two couples go out together. I decided to go, and we all went to the Paramount Theatre on Broadway to see *The Young Lions*. This was a picture about Nazi Germany, and it was a subject that really interested me. Marlon Brando was playing a Nazi Officer with blond hair. At that time Marlon Brando was a favorite of all the girls. Of course, he was slim and handsome then. The date went okay, but I wasn't enthralled with Jim or his friends. We did not go out again for a few months, and then one Friday night, I met him on the subway again. He was making casual conversation with me, and I liked the way he smiled. I thought this guy really likes me. He asked me what I was doing over the weekend, and I said, "Nothing." He said, "How would you like to go to the movies?" I thought, "Why not, I am not doing anything" … so I said, "Okay." I can remember exactly what I wore that night. It was a beautiful light pink silk dress which, naturally, my mother had made, and I was wearing my new bone color heels. When Jim arrived, he was all dressed up, shirt, tie, etc. That was the way he always was, beautifully dressed. We began to walk to the movies, and we walked and walked and talked all the way to the Kings Theatre which was about two miles from my house. The time went by so fast, and we had such a great conversation that I thought, "Hmmm, this could be the start of something big." In those days, the movie houses were very opulently appointed, and many of them had the word "palace" on the marquee. For instance, a movie theatre would be called the "Loew's Palace." I think the theatres were designed to let the moviegoer experience the thrill of really going someplace special. This particular movie house was all decorated in red carpeting with gold banisters and red velvet couches. Because the movie, *Vertigo* starring Jimmy Stewart and Kim Novak, had already begun when we got there, and they were not allowing anyone in after the picture started because it was a mystery with an unusual ending, Jim and I sat on one of the many couches in the theatre and continued our conversation. Time just flew by, and I think we both knew that we were compatible. After the movie, we went out for something to eat or drink, I'm not sure, and then we walked all the way home. It wasn't that Jim wouldn't spring for a taxi, but it was a beautiful night, and we were having a great time.

That was the beginning of a beautiful friendship. Jim and I have been friends for about 50 years now, and we always have something to say to each other. We knew that this would be the case the first night we took that walk to the movies. We continued to go out … nothing serious … on and off for a long time.

I think I knew that I was becoming attached to Jim when I decided to knit him a pair of argyle socks. In Brooklyn, in my high school, the girls who had a steady boyfriend always made them argyle socks. These socks were very hard to make, and I never would make them for anyone I wasn't seriously interested in because it was a very time consuming task, and I wanted to be sure that whoever got them was going to appreciate all my labor. But I always wanted to make a pair, so I bought a kit and decided I would make a pair for Jim. To explain, argyle socks are a plaid design, and it requires many bobbins of thread to make the socks. The whole package was sold in a kit which came with the thread, the bobbins, the needles and directions.

I had never knitted much, but I was confident I could do this. I carried my kit with me all the time and whenever I had a free moment, like during the subway ride to and from work, I would work on the socks. In the subway, one usually saw the same people, so most of the people in my car observed me making these socks over a period of time. The sock started off with the ribbing at the top of and ended at the toe.

As I continued to knit, day after day, an elderly Jewish lady on the train was observing me. She obviously knew how to knit, and one day she had finally had enough of watching me knit this monster size sock, and she came over and spoke to me. She said, "Dahling, you are not doing it right. The foot of the sock is too long … the upper part of the sock should be longer than the foot." I looked up at her, and then explained that my boyfriend wore a size 13 shoe and a 14 sock. She said she was sorry, but she had never seen a sock that size. To make a long story short, I made these socks without Jim ever seeing them. He was thrilled when I gave him his present. No one had ever made him a pair of socks before. He loved them, and then one weekend we went to the country, and Tom and Rosemary were there. Rosemary insisted she would wash the socks for Jim, and she did, and she shrunk them. Jim could never wear them again, and I was horrified. That was the end of my sock-making career.

Jim was now very interested in me, but I still wasn't sure, as he hadn't finished college, and I was determined to marry a man who graduated from college. My father expected this of me, as my brothers had graduated from college and he wanted me to meet a man like my brothers.

In spite of the fact that Jim was not a college graduate, my father really liked him, and he had more in common with him than he had with his sons. Jim was into baseball, football, prize fighting, and these were all the things he could talk about with my father.

When Jim realized how serious I was about the "college graduate thing," he decided to go to college. Since he was very smart, getting into Brooklyn College was not a problem for him. He went for a year to Pace College, and then transferred to Brooklyn College. At that time, Brooklyn College had a great reputation and was very difficult to get into, but he did it, and he went free to college.

When Jim started college, we spent a lot of time, especially on Sundays after dinner, visiting the Brooklyn Library and the Brooklyn Museum. Jim did whatever studying he needed to do in the Brooklyn Library, while I perused the fiction shelves.

My mother began inviting Jim to Sunday dinner. Since she was making this Sunday dinner anyway, she always said to me, "Call Jim for dinner." So my Mom, Dad, Jim and I spent many Sunday afternoons at dinner. My mother loved Jim because he was a perfect guest, and he loved having dinner at our house. It is always fun to cook for someone who appreciates your dinner. Jim and I almost always went out on Friday after work in the city, and we would walk all over. In those days, I could walk from 42nd street to Central Park which was at 57th Street in my three-inch pointy toe heels and think nothing of it. Actually, we often walked that trip to Central Park to have lunch.

On Saturdays, we always went dancing in Brooklyn. Dancing was our favorite thing, and we are perfectly in sync when we dance. It takes years of practice to dance like we do, but we practiced for five years before we got married.

We were in no rush as life was fun and there was no pressure on us to get married. Actually for the first three years, we were just "hanging around" having fun. I don't think I quite realized how determined Jim was to marry me, but I was beginning to see that he was serious when he met me every morning at the train station, and we traveled to work together. Then we went to lunch together almost every day, and then we rode home on the train every evening. We always had something to say to each other, and we never argued … we just enjoyed each other's company. Since we worked in the same company, we never let anyone know we were dating. It just wasn't done in those days ... mixing business and pleasure.

A funny thing happened one day when a friend of mine, Betty O'Connor, and I went to lunch. We stopped at the shoemaker to get my shoe fixed. Those were the days of the really skinny high heel and they always had to be repaired (shoemakers hated them), so I spent a lot of time in this particular shoe repair shop. The shoemaker, a little old Italian man, who knew me very well, asked me, "When are you going to marry that guy?" I looked at him like he was crazy and Betty O'Connor, who had no clue I was going out with Jim, asked me what he was talking about. I told her he was confused. Actually, the shoemaker was a romantic, and had seen Jim and me so many times in his shop and passing his shop that he was wondering when I was going to say "yes" to someone who was obviously so interested in me.

Many people seemed to know that I would marry Jim. One of my dearest friends, Kathleen Gibbons, met us one day early in our courtship in Macy's Department Store. It was the first time she had met Jim, although I had told her about him. She called me the next day and said, "You're going to marry that guy." She said she could tell he was "nuts about me." To this day, I think the best man to marry is the one "who is nuts about you."

I never really dated anyone until I met Jim. I had gone out a few times, but if I met someone and he was even potentially someone I wouldn't think of marrying, I never went out with him again. When we were in school, the nuns told us never to get involved with someone we couldn't potentially marry. That meant he had to be a Catholic and an upstanding man. I took that advice to heart. I had met two upstanding men in my life, my Dad and my Uncle Chris, so I knew what I was looking for. Jim had all these qualities. The things he was missing were money and a college education. As I said earlier, he remedied the college education part of the equation, and then he set about being successful.

I had told him I wouldn't consider marrying him because I was making more money than he was. That didn't bother him. It was just one more obstacle to overcome. He went about becoming a salesman for the Martex Towel Company. He took a personality test to see if he had the skills necessary to be a salesman, and he scored higher than the head of the sales division. After taking that test, he was on his way. With Jim's new position, he had more money to spend on things like theatre tickets and dining out. We loved to go to Broadway shows and we did this to celebrate all occasions like birthdays, etc. Broadway was at its best in the 1950s and the prices were within the reach of most everyone. Today the prices are so ridiculous that the average person cannot see a

Broadway show, but we saw them all. And we saw them with the great actresses and actors. For instance, just before Jim left for his new job in Cincinnati, we went to see *Camelot* with Richard Burton, Julie Andrews and Robert Goulet. It was the first time I had seen Richard Burton, and he was a phenomenal actor. When he came on stage, everyone else disappeared. He had what is called "charisma" to the max. When I saw him, I was so taken with him that I said to Jim, "No wonder Elizabeth Taylor left Eddie Fisher." At that time, the great scandal was that Elizabeth Taylor and Richard Burton were "an item." We saw *My Fair Lady* with Rex Harrison and Julie Andrews, and *Gypsy* with Ethel Merman. I can't remember them all, but these were great evenings.

I remember one birthday of mine when we didn't go out because it was snowing like crazy. Instead we were going to celebrate at my house with my parents. We took the train home, as usual, but instead of getting off at Franklin Avenue (my stop), we got off at the Brooklyn Museum stop so that we could have a romantic walk through the Brooklyn Botanical Gardens on the way home. We were walking in the gardens when the snowstorm turned into a blizzard. We could not see where we were going, and because Jim was wearing glasses, it was doubly difficult, as the glasses were coated with sleet and snow. What should have been a ten minute walk through the park took an hour, and we really thought we were going to wind up frozen to death in a snow bank.

Jim and I had been going out for about three years when I decided to go to Europe with my friend, Kathleen. I had promised I would go with Kathleen, and even though it was going to cost a lot of money which I could have saved for the day I got married, I could not go back on my word. Kathleen was really looking forward to the trip and I couldn't disappoint her. Jim was not too happy about this, but he said it was my decision to make. Another thing he was not happy about at this time was my new haircut. I had my hair cut in the "poodle cut" style. Jim hated it to say the least. He loved my long hair and he thought the hair cut was horrible. I actually thought it looked quite good.

Kathleen and I went on our "grand tour." We flew to Madrid first. This was a sixteen hour trip in a propeller plane. We were sitting three across, and it was very cramped for these sixteen-hours. The plane stopped once in Newfoundland to refuel. This was really the dark ages of flying. No jets in those days. After Spain, we went to Rome, then to Venice, Paris and we ended up in Ireland. We decided to skip London, as we had met an obnoxious British woman on our travels who was very anti-American. Actually, she was a Canadian and went on and on about how the Canadians really were the ones who helped win World War II. We decided after meeting her that we really didn't want anything to do with the British.

I remember that we landed in Madrid on a Sunday at about 6 a.m. The first thing we did after we got to our hotel was go to Mass. There were no kneelers in the church, and everyone seemed to be walking around saying their rosaries right in the middle of the Mass. It was very different from Sunday Mass in the United States. In the United States, people paid attention; in Spain all the women were intent on saying their rosaries. I might mention here that the church was full of women, mostly dressed in black. There were very few men in church. I believe it was a culture thing. The women went to church to pray for the men, who seemed to be standing outside of the church smoking.

The next thing we did was have breakfast in the hotel dining room. I remember this very vividly because the eggs came floating to the table in a sea of olive oil. This is not good, I thought. I could never eat this stuff … it was too greasy. But the real reason I remember this breakfast is that when we went outside in the street I realized that my wallet with all my cash, and my passport, was not in my pocketbook. I panicked because this was the first day of the trip, and without money or a passport, I was stuck. I ran back into the hotel and tried to explain to the maître d' about the situation, and it wasn't easy because English was not as widely understood as it is today, and I didn't know any Spanish. Finally, he grasped what I was saying and he told a busboy about the wallet. The busboy dove under the long white tablecloth which covered the table to the floor, and there was the wallet just laying there. I thought it was a miracle, and thanked God profusely for returning the wallet to me. I was so excited that I gave the busboy a twenty dollar bill. He was so excited by the huge tip that he hugged me. In those days, in Madrid, everything was so cheap that $20.00 would be like $100 today. He was jumping up and down with glee. The whole scenario caused quite a commotion in the hotel; Kathleen and I had made a grand entrance.

We did the usual tourist things in Madrid for about three days. Of course, we went shopping, as all things made of leather were so inexpensive there. We bought beautiful leather gloves, and I remember buying a pair of white kid leather gloves which I was going to wear at my wedding. I also bought a mantilla which I was going to use for a wedding veil. As you can see, I had every confidence that

when I returned from this trip, I was going to get married.
I also bought a beautiful gold charm in Spain for my
charm bracelet. Charm bracelets were all the rage in
1950s. My Dad had given me this gold bracelet for my
21st birthday, and I was about to embark on the job of
buying a charm from every country I visited.

After about three days of eating the Spanish food which
we found difficult as we had never seen it before and we
were used to meat and potatoes (Irish food), we met two
fellows who were in the U.S. Air Force. They invited us
out to dinner, and we jumped at the chance to dine at the
U.S. Officers' Club where we could get an American steak
and a baked potato. I can't remember anything about
these guys except the dinner was delicious.

We had purchased the airplane ticket to the farthest point
in our journey which was determined to be Madrid. After
that, we could fly back to the United States stopping
anywhere along the plane route. Our next stop was
Rome. Geographically, this does not make sense because
Rome is farther away from New York than Madrid, but
that is how the ticket was sold and it worked for us. We
saw every museum and church in Rome; we ate Italian
food in quaint restaurants, and Kathleen and I said we
were the only two American girls who were never pinched
in Rome. It seems that Italian men love to pinch
American girls, but it never happened to us. Anyway, if
someone did pinch us, we would never have known
because we always wore a girdle in those days. That was a
crazy thing, as we were so slim, we didn't need a girdle,
but it was just the way things were then. After Rome, we
went to Venice. Venice was spectacular and the most
unusual place I have ever been. It was a very romantic
city, but we couldn't appreciate it fully. One should

always be in a gondola with one's husband, and not one's girlfriend.

Then we went on to Paris for more touring. Touring in Paris was a great experience. They were all geared up for tourists, as was Rome, with designated language buses (English, Italian, etc.) so that the guide on an "English" bus only spoke English. During the day, we saw every museum and Cathedral and at night, we went to nightclubs.

We met some interesting guys on the nightclub tour. They were from New Zealand, and were on the "Grand Tour." We were amazed to hear that they were on a six month vacation. We asked them, "Why, so long?" and they said, "Once you get out of New Zealand, you have to do whatever you are going to do because you will probably never come back … it's too far."

And then we were off to Ireland. Kathleen had never been to Ireland and she loved it. We both "fit in" in Ireland. Everyone there was just like us and they looked like us, and we felt that we had reached "home."

We rented a car, and off we went to Galway. I was the driver. Kathleen was amazed that I could drive there and she thought several times that we were going to be killed. It is a genuine experience to drive in Ireland on the left hand side of the road. We had some close calls, but we made it.

As Kathleen only had a few days left of her vacation, the first place we went was to Galway to see Kathleen's relatives. They lived in a village, and it was so small, about eight houses, that we blew right through the village before realizing we were in and out of it. I turned the car around, and all these people (from the eight houses) were standing in the road to welcome us. They were so glad to see us they dragged me out of the car and began kissing me and welcoming me and saying I looked just like them. They just assumed that since I was the driver, I was their relative. I had to tell them that I was not their cousin, and that Kathleen was. This was all very funny when they thought about it because Kathleen looked just like them. They were the most charming people. They were very simple, had few material possessions, but for the two nights we stayed there, they entertained us royally. Each night, they all gathered and had a ceili which is an Irish party with singing and dancing. They had a fiddler who played wonderful music and we all danced country Irish dances. They were amazed at how Irish Kathleen and I were and how we could dance. Of course, Kathleen was a champion Irish step dancer in the United States, and they knew that. So Kathleen had to get up each night and show them her stuff. She could do everything, hornpipes, reels, jigs, etc. The first night after Kathleen finished dancing they had me get up and do a "jig." Of course, following Kathleen's act was like following Fred Astaire. So the next night, I decided I would dance first so that I wouldn't look so bad in comparison to Kathleen.

These ceilis were held in the kitchens of these houses. All the furniture was moved back and we all started doing set dancing. The young men actually swung Kathleen and me off our feet. We were flying through the air, but we were able to do it, as all we ever did in Brooklyn was dance, and we were able to dance with anyone who could lead us. It was great fun.

One of the things I did while on my trip to Europe with Kathleen was take pictures. The pictures were all on 35 millimeter slides, and although it was a real effort to stop my sightseeing to take these pictures, they ultimately proved to be a great source of entertainment years later when my children were small. Once a year, I would drag out the slide projector and the slides and show the children the pictures which I had taken all over Europe. They loved to look at these pictures of Rome, Venice, Paris, Ireland and Germany. The boys were particularly intrigued with the slides of the bullfights I saw in Spain. I explained to them how the tickets to the bullfights were priced according to whether you wanted to sit in the shade or in the sunshine. The tickets for the shady side were more expensive. Years later two of my sons went to Madrid to see the bullfights, and they remembered that they wanted to sit on the shady side of the arena. These slide shows really expanded their minds and fostered in them, or at least a couple of them, a great desire to travel and see Europe. These slides proved to be a classic example of the age old wisdom that many of the best things in life are the simple things you can do for yourself.

Anyway, after we left Kathleen's relations, we went back to Dublin where Kathleen boarded her plane to go home and I met my aunt and uncle for tea in the Gresham Hotel. High Tea is an experience not to be missed in Ireland. I also went to the All Ireland Football Championship game in Dublin with my uncles, and almost got trampled to death. In Irish football stadiums, there were no seats at that time. Everyone stood on the side of a hill and watched this wild game. When the game was over, everyone proceeded down the hill to go through a narrow gate to get out of the field. I was walking down the hill to the gate when suddenly I felt myself being picked up by my two uncles and carried in this mass of people through the gate. I think if they didn't pick me up,

I would have fallen and would have been trampled to death. I have never forgotten that experience.

After visiting in Waterford for another week with my relatives, whom I thoroughly enjoyed, I flew home.

I can remember wondering what would happen with Jim. Was he still going to be interested in me?

I was beginning to think that maybe I had been too hasty just going on this trip and blowing Jim off. However, when I returned to my house, there was this huge bouquet of red roses sitting there waiting for me, and I knew the romance was still on. When I called Jim at his house to tell him I was home and to thank him for the flowers, he obviously had someone visiting. He said he wanted to see me and would be over in a couple of hours. I guess it took him that long to bring his new-found girlfriend home to her house.

When Jim and I got together, I think we decided to stop fooling around and get serious about the future. From that time, we kept "steady company." "Steady company" was an expression of my father's. He always asked me if my friends had an understanding and were they keeping "steady company." That meant were they seriously considering marriage.

Since Jim and I were now at the stage where we had "an understanding" and were "keeping steady company," I began to seriously think about changing my job, as it was not considered a good idea to date someone in your office. Fortunately, at this time, I was offered a job in the Dodge News Bureau, a division of the Chrysler Corporation.

The administrative assistant position that Dodge offered was a step up from the secretarial position I currently held and the salary was significantly better. Due to an autoworkers union contract clause, I would receive a "cost-of-living" bonus every three months in addition to the base salary. All Chrysler employees in the New York office were entitled to the same benefits as the union employees in Detroit. There were all sorts of other perks, so I took the job.

It turned out to be a crazy experience, as the man I worked for was a very strange individual. He didn't really need a secretary because he typed all his own letters using the "hunt and peck" system, and he was as fast as any secretary. The only thing he wanted me to do was type envelopes. That was really weird. He was head of the east coast division of the Dodge News Bureau, and he was responsible for getting favorable press coverage on Dodge Cars and Trucks.

In addition to typing envelopes, my main responsibilities were answering the telephone and telling people, "Mr. Smith is not in" and arranging press parties. Press parties were opportunities for mixing with members of the press and for handing out press releases on the new line of Dodge vehicles. In today's vernacular, I would have been considered an "Event Planner." These affairs had generous budgets from the Chrysler Corporation and were very lavish.

Another aspect of this job was arranging to have an array of cars parked in a New York garage and making them available for members of the press to use at their discretion. It was my responsibility to order six new cars every three months. I could order these cars just as easily as I could order office supplies. To do this, I would fill out a separate order form for each car, and I could order anything I wanted. I would order a station wagon, a convertible and several sedans for the use of the press. It was fun. I picked out the color of the cars, options, and then the color and material of the interior. Most times, my boss didn't change what I ordered and just signed off on the form. However, one day, he had a fit because I ordered a green car. He screamed at me that I should know that no automotive man would drive a green car. "It was hard luck." I remember thinking, "How would I know that?" Needless to say, that was the last time I ever ordered a green car at Dodge; and it was years before I owned a green car myself.

While I was working at Dodge, I got my friend Betty a job there as well. We both worked on the 56th Floor, of the Chrysler Building. At that level, the Chrysler Building swayed when the wind blew. Betty didn't like this, and whenever it was a particularly windy day, Betty and I took the elevator down to the 1st floor for a cup of coffee at Schrafft's. My boss objected to this, but I told him we were "entitled" to two 15 minute coffee breaks per day in accordance with the union contract. Since there was no place on the 56th floor to take a coffee break, we had to go down to the 1st floor, and that trip, in those old elevators, took some time. We therefore decided to take our coffee break starting when we got off the elevator. Mr. Smith wasn't too happy about that.

Many strange things happened to me while I worked for Mr. Smith. He was a bundle of nervous energy and tension. He never walked; he always ran around the office. He wore a dirty raincoat, winter and summer. I think he thought this affectation made him look like a newsman. One day, I was sitting at my desk in the outer office when I heard a crashing noise coming from the inner office. It was my boss throwing his telephone book across the room. He had gotten so frustrated with the telephone company and their new all numeric dialing system that he finally "flipped his lid."

Up until this time phone numbers had consisted of a telephone exchange name, such as Butterfield 8, followed by a short phone number. This made it easy to remember frequently called numbers. Now the phone company was introducing fully numeric phone numbers consisting of an area code and a seven-digit number. It was more than my boss could take.

To express his displeasure with this change, Mr. Smith would dial the long distance operator and say he wanted to be connected to nine billion, seven hundred and thirty-seven million, eight hundred and thirty-four thousand, nine hundred and eight. After he repeated this several times to the befuddled operator, she usually disconnected him. He ended up throwing the telephone book across the room. I put on my hat and went home. This day, I had finally had enough of his antics, and I intended to quit.

When I arrived home I called the head office in Detroit to tell them I was leaving the company. I spoke to the Director of Public Relations and he said he would call me back. A short time later, he called and asked me not to quit. He assured me that I would never have any more trouble with my boss. When I arrived at work the next day, Mr. Smith told me that if he did anything to make me quit, he would be fired. It wasn't an apology. It was a statement of fact. He wasn't happy to be in this situation and a short time later he left Dodge.

He was replaced by a great guy, Moon Mullins, and we got along fine. After eighteen months, I left Dodge on the Thursday before my wedding. Before I departed, I recommended a good friend of mine for my job, and she stayed in this position for many years and she eventually retired from Dodge.

All the perils of my secretarial exploits didn't affect my personal life, and Jim and I continued going out. Jim continued to go to college and then before we knew it, it was my 27th birthday. Naturally, we went out somewhere special to celebrate, and then we came home. The next morning my father was expecting to see an engagement ring, and when he didn't, he asked me, "What are Jim's intentions?" I conveyed that message to Jim the next evening, and the following day we visited a jeweler we knew in Greenwich Village, and had an engagement ring made. Jim brought the jeweler his own diamond and the jeweler set it in a yellow gold high Tiffany setting.

My birthday was March 3rd and on March 17th, we got engaged. First, we went to the Village to pick up the ring and then to celebrate the occasion, we went on a whirlwind trip of the city. I remember that it was a Friday night, and so the restaurant would have to be a fish house of some sort. But the first place we went was downtown to the Wall Street area and a restaurant called Fraunces Tavern, where Jim actually proposed and gave me the ring. Jim picked this place because it was a very well known historical site and we were into historical sites. This tavern was the place where George Washington gave his farewell address to his troops. It probably seems like a strange place to get engaged, but it was a very charming place, and Jim really loved it.

After that, we went to the fish restaurant where we had dinner. We met two ladies in this restaurant who admired my beautiful ring. Then we went to the Top of the Sixes, one of our favorite spots … very romantic, and located at

666 Fifth Avenue. After a couple of drinks there, we ended up the evening by going to a jazz club … one of Jim's favorite things.

I actually went to the jazz club because Jim was really into jazz, and still is, but I don't like jazz, and told Jim that night that I didn't like jazz. He wasn't too happy with that; but love is blind. It was a great, happy night, and I remember it as if it were yesterday.

Portrait taken on my 27th birthday March 3rd 1962

It Only Happens Now and Then …

The next day, when I woke up, I showed my Mom and Dad the ring. They were quite happy that I had got engaged; I think they were beginning to wonder would it ever happen. Since I was now 27, I think my Dad was afraid I was going to be "left on the shelf," meaning that I would end up an old maid.

However, my Dad was disappointed that Jim hadn't spoken to him first before he asked me to marry him. That was the way it was usually done. Jim and I made a mistake there; but since my Dad had asked what Jim's intentions were, and Jim immediately declared his intentions by getting the ring, I think Jim and I felt that my Dad was telling Jim "to get moving on this engagement" and therefore, he approved, which he did. My Dad really liked Jim, as did my Uncle Chris.

Since my parents really believed in long courtships (ours was about six years) and short engagements, we made plans to be immediately married, and we were married seven months later on October 20th, 1962.

Before we could get married, we had to find a place to live, and I flew to Cincinnati where Jim was living and working as a salesman for Martex Towels. It was the first time I had ever flown anywhere in the United States. I had been to Europe, but had never been out of the eastern part of the United States. It was a great adventure. I stayed at the house of Jim's boss, Ed Knight. Ed and his wife, Muriel, were so gracious to us. We spent the weekend looking for an apartment, and we found one in Bond Hill, a suburb of Cincinnati. It was owned by an elderly German couple, and it was spotless. It had two bedrooms, a large living room and dining area and a small, but workable kitchen. We were thrilled, as the price was right, and we would never have found such a nice apartment in Brooklyn. I was very impressed with Cincinnati. It was such a clean city, very different from Brooklyn. There was no litter anywhere. I attributed that to the fact that there were so many Germans living in Cincinnati.

The next thing to be done was to get the furniture. I thought I could do this by myself as I knew people who were in the furniture business and who were interior decorators, so I had entrée to the furniture showrooms in New York. I thought buying the furniture would be easy, and so Betty Keane and I set off one Saturday to pick out the furniture. I was overwhelmed by the selection of fabric, and could not make up my mind about what fabric to put on the couch. I was surprised that I was so indecisive about the color and texture of the materials. There were silks, damasks and cotton. I was overwhelmed, and it was something that I just couldn't decide without Jim, as it was very important to me that Jim like it. He had excellent taste, so I decided to wait until he came to New York. Thank God, Jim was coming to town for a business meeting.

He looked at the fabrics, picked out what he liked and that is what we bought. It was a great decision, and we lived with that couch and chair for about 20 years, and never tired of the design.

Back to Cincinnati Jim went, and the next time I saw him was the Thursday before the wedding.

Jim went with me to Lord & Taylor to pick up my gown. In those days, in the city, wedding gowns were packed in wonderful big boxes with lots of tissue paper and a wonderful white ribbon around the box. As you can imagine, the box was huge, and it really needed a man to carry it. So there we were, the two of us, once again on the subway, with this precious package. On the day before the wedding I had my hair done, and on the morning of the wedding, I just combed my hair and off I went to the church. In those days, there was no elaborate preparation of one's hair and make-up as there is today. I also remember that it was the first time I had a manicure.

A couple of days before my wedding, my brother, Joseph, flew in from Germany, and it was a surprise. We weren't sure that he would make it, but he said, "I would never miss my only sister's wedding." We were so happy to see each other. Joseph and I had always been kindred spirits. During the course of his whirlwind visit, he surprised us with the news that he, too, was getting married. He hadn't said anything before because he didn't want to take the spotlight from my wedding. He told us he had met this lovely, petite American school teacher in Germany, Edith Parkin, and they were planning to marry in December. We were all so surprised by the announcement, as we thought Joseph would be a bachelor for years. He did get married in Germany, in December of 1962, and we met Edie the following year when they returned to the United States. Edie was a great addition to the family. She was a charming girl from California, and she has been one of us for 48 years now.

I can remember the day of my wedding so clearly. It was a beautiful October day; the sun was shining and the temperature was in the high 80s. I remember thinking "Is it too hot for my heavy formal silk dress?" But it was autumn, not summer, and so, even though the day was warm, it was clear with no humidity and the weather was not a problem.

Before the wedding, I was very concerned because I was moving to Cincinnati, Ohio, and I would be leaving my mother and father behind in Brooklyn. At first, it seemed like a great adventure to go to Cincinnati to start my married life, but that was when my brother Tom was living in New Jersey.

Unfortunately, right before the wedding he was transferred to Massachusetts, and therefore, he was also leaving the area. My brother Joseph was making a career as an officer in the Army, and he would be traveling all around the world. I felt very sad about leaving my parents. It just didn't seem right to me. They were great about it; they never once expressed any sadness about my going, but I knew they were sad to see their only daughter going so far away.

My mother was so nervous about the whole thing that I remember going to the family doctor and talking to him about it, and he said my mother and I should take a very mild tranquilizer the day of the wedding and so we did. We laughed when we took the tranquilizer because we had never done anything like this before, but the doctor said it was such a little dosage, it wouldn't affect us at all. Now that I look back on it, it was probably a placebo, but whatever it was, we sailed through the day and had a wonderful time.

When we got to the church, and I arrived at the altar to meet Jim, I can remember clearly what he said to me. He leaned over, and with this great charming smile on his face, he said, "Is that a new dress you're wearing?" I immediately smiled at him, and that was the beginning of a great day and a great journey through life.

Arriving at the church with my father

Just married!

Dancing the first dance at our wedding reception

Traveling in the style of a by-gone era

The wedding reception was in the Fort Hamilton Officers' Club in the Bay Ridge section of Brooklyn. We had a wonderful orchestra and they played all our favorite dance tunes ... all the classics. Even though we were in the "Sixties," Jim and I always liked, and still do, the great old standard tunes. Jim picked out the song for the first dance and it was from the movie *Gigi* ... *Thank Heaven for Little Girls*. What a great uplifting song to start the wedding. We had the whole floor to ourselves and danced from one end of it to the other with great joy.

Then I danced with my father who was also a beautiful dancer. He requested a waltz in three-quarter time ... he knew exactly what type of music he wanted to dance to. He did this marvelous waltz that he called the "Twinkle Waltz." It had some very interesting steps in it, but it was no problem for me because I had been waltzing with my father for years, and I knew exactly what he was doing. That is such a fond memory.

After the wedding reception, Jim and I left to go to the airport, and fly to New Orleans, Louisiana where we spent ten days on our honeymoon. We decided to go to New Orleans because it was a very cosmopolitan city, and we considered ourselves "cosmopolitan," although I am sure we weren't terribly cosmopolitan.

When we arrived in New Orleans, it was so hot and humid that I was horrified, as I had all fall clothing with me and I was not prepared for the humidity. The next day Jim remedied this by taking me out shopping and buying me a lightweight blouse that tided me over for just one day because the forecast was for cool weather. Fortunately, the next day the weather changed, and I was "back in business" with the proper trousseau. That was very important to me.

Anyway, we stayed in the French Quarter in a charming place called the Maison de Ville in the Court of the Two Sisters. This place was indeed charming and full of atmosphere, but had very little hot water and no television. After spending three nights here, and coming home very late in the evening, and seeing these immense water bugs scurrying around the courtyard, Jim decided he had had enough of "atmosphere," so he called American Express and arranged for us to move to the Hotel Monteleone for the rest of our stay. As a traveling salesman, Jim was used to staying where the showers were hot, the rooms were carpeted and there were no water bugs. He was happy, and I was happy, because I had had the atmosphere experience, and I preferred the full service hotel with a restaurant, night club, etc. I guess we were cosmopolitan after all.

One of the fun things about the Hotel Monteleone was the fact that they had a carousel bar. This is a bar that revolves around. One night Jim and I stopped for a nightcap there and Jim got off the carousel to use the men's room. When he came back to the spot where he left me I wasn't there, and he was very upset until he remembered that the bar was revolving, and I was now on the other side of the room. He said "Wow, I have to stop drinking."

When we were taxiing from the Court of the Two Sisters to the Hotel Monteleone, the driver asked us, "What do you think of the war?" "What war?" Jim responded. As we had had no TV at the Court of the Two Sisters, we did not know that the U.S. was about to invade Cuba; and that Cuba was not too far from New Orleans.

Everyone in New Orleans, except Jim and me, was really concerned about the "war." Anyway, the taxi driver was appalled by our lack of knowledge about the "war," and he threw his newspaper back at us and said, "Read this, you need it more than I do" … and that is how we found out about the Cuban Missile Crisis. We did not let the "war" interfere with our honeymoon. We went blissfully along dining and dancing our way through New Orleans.

The night life in New Orleans was great. People dined there at 9 p.m. in the evening, which was fine with us. Our schedule of activities included sleeping late in the morning, having a great breakfast, which, on occasion included Brandy Alexanders, and then taking in the sights. We saw all the Civil War sites, visited the ante bellum mansions and walked through cemeteries where people were entombed above the ground because New Orleans is below sea level. The guides in New Orleans were really into the history of the city, and were always happy to discuss all aspects of life in New Orleans. It is a fascinating place, or at least it was then before Katrina, the hurricane.

After a day of sightseeing, we went back to our hotel, took a rest and proceeded to get ready for evenings on the town. I think we went to every great restaurant in New Orleans, but to tell the truth, I did not like the food. I loved the idea of dining out and I loved the ambiance and the romance of it all, but the food, in my opinion, left a lot to be desired. Jim, on the other hand, loved the food. Invariably, we would order something that I had never heard of before, and the waiter would bring it to the table, and I couldn't eat it. It was too rich for me, too exotic, etc. I am such a plain eater that I just couldn't adjust to the cuisine. So I would say to Jim, "Pass the bread, please" (the bread was GREAT). Finally, after a few nights of passing the bread to me, Jim said, "Mary, this bread is costing me a fortune."

After dinner, which lasted until midnight, we would go out for dancing and drinks and then finally wind up in the Café du Monde, which was open all night, and frequented by people from all walks of life. You would see workmen in there in their overalls, and you would see revelers in white tie and tails. New Orleans is a city where people are always partying. In the Café du Monde, they made wonderful chicory coffee, of course, plus the most delicious beignets coated with powdered sugar … so delicious and fattening … but since I wasn't eating any food, I didn't gain any weight.

We usually got back to our hotel at around four in the morning, and we were not the only ones returning at that time. People were really out late in that city.

The next day, we would do the same thing all over again; that is, we would do some major sightseeing during the day, rest in the late afternoon, and go out on the town.

When the honeymoon was over, we flew back to Cincinnati, Ohio, where we began our married life.

Early Married Life

First of all, I want to say that I loved married life. I loved having my own home which I set out to decorate with a vengeance. I had never had an opportunity to do any decorating before, as I had always lived with my parents until my marriage.

As an aside, I must tell you how at one time during my secretarial career in New York City, I decided I would get a studio apartment in the city. Many other girls did that, and so I thought, why not me? When I broached this subject with my father, he calmly told me there were only two ways I was leaving his house, and one was in a wedding dress and the other was in a box. So, that was the last time I mentioned this to my father. As a matter of fact, the girls in my crowd all went from their parents' home to their husband's home when they married. It was very different from today.

Regarding married life in Cincinnati, since I was not working (I retired the Thursday before the wedding, thank God. I had worked long enough (9 years), and now I was going to do what I was meant to do … be a wife and mother), I was very serious about making a home for Jim and me. Every day, I would go shopping for the house, curtains, pots & pans, rugs, etc. It was great fun. We had a comfortable amount of money, which we got as wedding gifts, and it was for spending. At least, in my mind, it was for spending and spend it I did. I had a charge account at Carew's in Cincinnati, and I blissfully signed my new name Mrs. James N. Hamilton to all sorts of sales slips.

Jim didn't mind what I did. He went off to work every day happy to have a wife who was in the business of taking care of him.

At first, we were in this routine where Jim and I would get up together, and he would go into the shower, and I would go into the kitchen to make his breakfast. At that time of the year, it was dark in Cincinnati at seven in the morning. I would make the coffee and then I would sit in the kitchen for an hour while Jim got ready for work. After a few days of this, I said to myself, "This is crazy, sitting here waiting for an hour for Jim to arrive in the kitchen." I then told Jim to wake me up when he finished the shower, and then I would proceed to the kitchen. That was my first good decision.

On the first day, before Jim left for work, I asked him what he would like for dinner. He calmly looked at me and said, "Mary, please don't ask me at 7:30 in the morning what I want for dinner. I haven't a clue. That's your job. Put something on the table, and I will eat it." I got the message that Jim didn't want to think about dinner, so I was on my own. What to do? I had never cooked dinner in my life. Of course, I had watched my mother make hundreds of dinners and so using my philosophy of "if someone else can make dinner, so can I," I proceeded to think about what my mother would do. I decided to go to the local butcher and explain to him that I didn't know what I was doing, but I would like to cook dinner. We settled on a roasting chicken, stuffed with potatoes and onion stuffing, just like my mother made. I got the usual things to go with it ... potatoes, carrots, etc., and off I went to open my cookbook and see how this was done.

Actually, it was easy to do this as we had roast chicken at least once a week in my parents' house. I also made a box cake; it was an apple crumb cake. Jim's boss's wife had told me about these cakes and I bought one on the way home, followed the directions and bingo, I was little Mary Homemaker. I set the table with all my great wedding gifts, and when Jim walked through the door at 6 p.m., he could smell the aroma of the chicken, and the apple cinnamon crumb cake, and he literally thought he had died and gone to heaven.

The best man to marry is a man who has been on his own for a while, and has been eating out. Somehow they really appreciate a wife who can cook and bake. Of course, Jim didn't really know that I didn't have a clue about shopping, cooking, baking or cleaning for that matter. All he knew was that when he arrived home, his wife had made him this great meal.

Since the first meal was such a success, I continued on a streak of luck. All I had to do to keep Jim happy was to go to the neighborhood butcher (who quickly became my best friend), pick out a piece of meat, get out my cookbook and whip up dinner. I didn't work outside the house and this was now my job, and I really loved being a homemaker. To this day, I am convinced that husbands who are fed are happy husbands.

Most of my days were spent shopping and decorating the apartment. I was great at decorating, but not so great at cleaning. I remember thinking that my mother had spoiled me, and if I ever had a daughter, I would teach her how to clean.

Jim and I lived in Cincinnati all by ourselves for about six months, and then we met a gal who had moved to Cincinnati from the Bronx. Her name was Mary

Stapleton, and I will never forget her. She was a most charming Irish girl, and I called her because Betty Keane's sister, Mary, who knew people all over the country insisted that she knew a gal in Cincinnati, and I should call her. So I did. What great fortune that was. Mary Stapleton had a whole group of friends, all from New York, and they welcomed us with open arms. We all did a lot of entertaining, as we were all newly married, and it was fun to entertain at home.

At about the same time we met this crowd, a young couple moved into the apartment next door. They were of German heritage, and we became great friends. He was a butcher and had come to America by way of Argentina. He was very good looking in a German way, tall and blonde, and he had the most charming German/Argentinean accent when he spoke English. Jim always maintained that he was probably the son of a U-boat commander who had been smuggled into Buenos Aires after the war. His wife's name was Linda. His name was Freddie Mueller.

They shared with us two great stories which we have never forgotten. I am putting them in the memoir because I enjoy telling these stories, and I want someone else to remember them.

The first story is about how Freddie met Linda.

Freddie worked for his uncle in a butcher shop in Cincinnati. Every Saturday a beautiful German girl, accompanied by an older German man, came to the shop to buy meat. The girl, Linda, was very shy and quiet and never said anything. One Saturday, she arrived at the shop all by herself. She wanted to buy one pork chop. Freddie said, "One pork chop?" What about your husband … doesn't he want a pork chop?"

She said, "I don't know what you're talking about, I'm not married." Freddie was so surprised that she was a single girl that he said, "Don't move." And with that, he took off his butcher's apron, and walked from behind the counter, and asked Linda to go out that night on a date. She was so shocked that she said, "Yes." That evening, they went to Coney Island, an amusement park in Cincinnati, and Freddie proposed. They were married in about three months, and it was a perfect match. Freddie always told us, "It was a match made in heaven."

The second story is about how Linda survived World War II.

One evening the four of us, Jim, Freddie, Linda and I were sitting around our living room talking about our youth, and Linda began to share with us the trials and tribulations of living in Germany during the war. She had never shared this story with anyone, including Freddie, but when she started to tell the story, she couldn't stop. It was as if she needed to tell the story, and she was going to do it all at once.

We sat there dumbfounded as she related the horrors of living under the Nazi regime for the next several hours. How I wished that I had a tape recorder so that I could have gotten it all down, but I will try to recall it as she told it to me.

Linda lived with her mother and little brother, who was about two, in a city in eastern Germany. I can't remember which one. Linda was about six years old at the time. She remembers that there were cars going around the city announcing that the Germans were winning the war, but her mother said that was impossible because they were starving. Linda's father was a soldier in the Wehrmacht, and he instructed Linda's mother to leave this town, take the two children and move west toward the American Army. He was going back to the Russian front, and he told her mother, they would never see him again, and they should leave as soon as he returned to the front. They stayed in their home a little while and then Linda's mother decided they would leave.

Linda told us she carried a pillowcase with some belongings in it and she said you could not believe how heavy that pillowcase became. She told us how she, her mother and little brother joined the hundreds of refugees trying to flee the city and the oncoming Russians. They walked for miles and miles, her mother carrying the baby, and Linda carrying the pillowcase. She said the road was littered with the possessions of the people who could no longer carry them. She particularly remembered sets of silver candlesticks, candelabra, etc., all the things that people thought they could sell to survive.

Eventually, Linda could no longer carry her pillowcase and she abandoned it also. Her mother walked on and on with the two children. At night they would sleep by the side of the road. Then her mother stole a horse and she put the two children on it and they walked on. It was winter at the time, and they had to cross a river. Linda's mother decided to wait until midnight to cross the river because although it looked like it was frozen, she wasn't sure. And she was right. People tried to cross the river in the daylight, and the ice cracked and they fell in. In the early morning, long after midnight, but before daylight, Linda's mother decided to make the trek across the river. She was successful, but when she got to the other side, someone stole the horse.

Now, she and the children were walking again. They had no food, and Linda's mother was trying to breastfeed the

156

baby. Finally, they made it to an embarkation point from where they would be able to cross to Sweden on a Red Cross ship. They missed the ship, and were told to wait for the next ship in a building which was like a glass airplane hangar. Her mother looked at this glass building and decided it really was not a safe shelter. She resolved they would not stay there, but would wait outside the building. Subsequently, the Red Cross ship which they missed (which was marked with a big red cross) was sunk leaving the harbor and the glass hangar was bombed in an air raid and most of the people inside were killed. Linda said it was a horrible sight.

Eventually, the trio made their way to a city in Sweden where the people were very generous to them. They provided clothes, food, lodging, etc. The baby was so frail that they decided to feed him milk and cheese, and his little body could not handle it after not having eaten anything for so long, and he died. In the end, all her mother's efforts to keep the boy alive were tragically to no avail. The journey was too hard. Linda and her mother were devastated.

Jim, Freddie and I were devastated.

Linda's father never returned from the Russian front, as he had predicted. Linda and her mother managed to survive, and after the war, they returned to Germany. When Linda was eighteen, she decided there was no future for her in Germany, and as she had studied some kind of photography in school, she decided to get a job in that field. At that time, there was a German photographer in Cincinnati who had advertised in the German papers for an assistant. She saw this ad, replied to it, and got the job. It took great courage to leave her mother at eighteen and travel to the United States. She could not speak any

English, and how she got to Cincinnati, I don't know, but she did. The man turned out to be a very reliable character, and even though he was years older than Linda, he was single and had an interest in marrying her. She had only worked for him six months when she met Freddie. He was young, handsome and charming, so she married him, and they were a perfect couple.

From Linda's story I learned that nothing turns people into pacifists more quickly than first-hand experience of the horrors of war.

A few years later, we met Linda's mother. She came to Cincinnati to meet her son-in-law. She was a wonderful woman, indomitable I would say. It was a pleasure to meet a woman of such courage. We could see where Linda got the strength to leave Germany at eighteen, travel to the U.S., and marry Freddie on the spur of the moment.

Adjusting to married life was not difficult for me. I didn't have to get to know Jim ... I knew him.

He was the same after we married as he was before except for the time he spent getting ready to go anyplace. Of course, I had never seen that, as he was always on time and ready when he came to my house to pick me up. But if this was the worst of his faults, it was no problem.

I have a few other stories of our early days in Cincinnati I would like to tell. I remember that on the first Halloween that Jim and I spent together, he asked me just before he left for work, what type of celebration I was planning for Halloween. I looked at him and said, "Celebration?" He said that his mother had always celebrated Halloween with some type of special decorations and dessert. I thought I better get my act together and figure something out. So that was the day I first learned to make cupcakes.

Off I went to the supermarket, bought a Duncan Hines cake mix, read the directions on the box, bought a cupcake tin and set about making these cupcakes. I frosted them with some kind of orange icing. I had mastered the art of the cupcake. Naturally, Jim thought he was married to "Betty Crocker."

The next big hurdle for me to overcome was Thanksgiving. I knew that Jim was expecting a great feast, as Thanksgiving is one of his favorite holidays. This was going to be a real challenge, because up to now, I had only been making simple dinners. I had never really cooked a full-fledged dinner such as I knew Jim was expecting. I had watched my mother cook, of course, but I was a frivolous spoiled young woman who had literally never done a thing in the kitchen, and now I was in Cincinnati, a long way from my "support group" in Brooklyn.

Although Jim and I had gone out for years, it never occurred to him that I couldn't just step into the kitchen and make this Thanksgiving Dinner with all the trimmings that he had had all his life. When I told him I didn't have a clue on where to start with this extravaganza, he was shocked. But he shouldn't have worried. Despite my lack of knowledge, I was determined to prepare this ceremonial dinner. We went shopping and bought all sorts of things that I had never heard of such as Brussels sprouts, lima beans, creamed onions and cranberry sauce in addition to the usual potatoes, carrots, string beans, stuffing, and of course, the bird.

I have to mention here that I only had three pots and a roasting pan in which to cook all these things. To this day, I am still using the same three pots, and I manage to cook all my dinners in these three pots plus a new roasting pan which is no mean feat considering I often cooked for a large family including four big sons.

Back to the story, on Thanksgiving Day, I labored all day in the kitchen to produce this meal while Jim, being the old fashioned guy that he was, read the paper and watched football.

One of the problems with the dinner was where to serve it. Since we were married less than a month, only some of our furniture had arrived. We had no dining room table, so we set up the two end tables and the coffee table for the feast. Out came the wedding gifts … the linen tablecloth and napkins, the silver, the china, and the Waterford Crystal. I must say here that Jim did set the table. He loved doing that, and to this day, Jim loves setting the table.

Eventually, after hours of "slaving over a hot stove," everything was ready, and we sat down, in solitary grandeur, to eat the meal. I, like the good little wife, passed the dishes one by one to Jim. He took a little of everything, and then I passed him the creamed onions.

He said, "No, thank you."

I said, "What do you mean, 'No thank you?'"

He replied, "I never eat creamed onions…"

I replied, "Then why did you have me make them?"

And, he said, "My mother always made creamed onions. My brother likes them."

So, there we sat and neither of us ate the creamed onions. Needless to say, creamed onions have never appeared on our Thanksgiving table again.

As I am writing this, I am thinking about my parents and how good they were to Jim and me. They gave us the china, the crystal, the silver, the linen tablecloths, and the money for the dining room furniture. I think they realized the importance of the dining room and the ritual of special dinners and especially the practice of eating together as a family in a nice atmosphere.

After the initial excitement of the honeymoon, and setting up housekeeping, I began to get homesick for my family and friends in Brooklyn. Telephoning was very expensive in those days, so I began to write letters detailing the adventures of married life.

As a salesman, Jim traveled on the road for two or three nights a week, and he wanted me to be able to "talk" to my friends, so one day he arrived home with a present for me. It was a typewriter. What a wonderful, thoughtful gift it was. I was thrilled because I could tell stories so much better by typing them rather than by writing them in longhand.

That typewriter saved my life. Letters were flying back and forth across the country. To this day, 45 years later, I am still corresponding with my dear friend Marie Farrell who started answering my letters all those years ago. She and I have been there for each other through some very difficult times. The saddest letter I ever wrote was on September 11, 2001 when she lost her beloved son John at the World Trade Center. Only a letter, and not a telephone call, could have conveyed the grief we felt at the loss of John.

I have written countless letters to my sons in college. I always found it easier to "talk to them" in a letter. They may not have wanted to hear what I had to say, but they were curious. Topics which I discussed included "not marrying in haste," "not dropping out of college," and "not losing their precious Catholic Faith," which I had passed on to them. Writing those letters worked for me. If I had started to speak to them about these matters they would say, "Later Mom ... I'm in a hurry." But a letter from your mother is quite rare these days, and its message is really read several times, so I think some of the words of wisdom actually do sink in.

It all started with the gift of the typewriter. If Jim hadn't thought to buy it for me all those years ago, I would never have gotten in the habit of writing letters. I think perhaps that the typewriter was the greatest gift I ever received.

Jim gave me two other gifts around this time that were more mundane, but which also proved invaluable. In a magazine I had around the house, he came across an article about the period of adjustment for newly married couples. The article stated that during the romantic stage of courtship, it is common to "attribute qualities to your partner that they do not possess." This phrase became an instant classic in our household and is still used by each of us at appropriate moments. Jim's first application of this concept was to give me two books pertaining to qualities he had attributed to me but that I clearly did not possess: *Heloise's Housekeeping Hints* by Heloise Bowles and Peg Bracken's humorous *I Hate to Cook Cookbook*. These books really saved me because in the early days of my marriage my homemaking skills were sorely lacking.

It actually took me all day, every day, to clean my house. I had no system, and I would start in the kitchen, and then get distracted and move to the bathroom. There was no order to how I cleaned the house. I should have paid more attention to my mother, but I don't recall that she had a system either. She was too busy sewing. Anyway, after I read *Heloise's Housekeeping Hints*, I realized that there was a system to housecleaning and I tried to follow her hints. I will be eternally grateful to Heloise as she made my life a little easier and Jim's life a little happier. I think homemaking skills should be taught at a very young age, so that they become totally routine. As for me, I did it because I had to, and because Jim is a very orderly man, but my natural inclination is to be a "clutterer." Years later, I solved the whole problem by getting a cleaning lady ... the greatest gift to the housewife.

As for the *I hate to Cook Cookbook*, I found recipes in there that got me through almost 50 years of marriage. They were wonder recipes, made for entertaining, and I have passed some of them along to my daughters-in-law. This book was just what I needed to entertain our new friends in Cincinnati. They were impressed with my culinary skills, but I could only invite them to dinner twice a year, because I only mastered two of the recipes.

For the first six months of our marriage, Jim and I didn't know a soul in Cincinnati except for Jim's boss and his wife. Jim and I got to be even better friends because there was no one else to hang around with. Our son, Jimmy, was born in Cincinnati. That was a traumatic experience for me because in those days, women just went to the hospital and had the baby. There was not a lot of preparation for having a baby. One just had the baby. Jim and I were very fortunate because Jimmy was born in a very short time. I think the whole process took about 3 1/2 hours. I had never been in a hospital before so it was actually very frightening. In that time, prospective fathers were not allowed to stay with their wives during the labor or delivery. So I was put in this dark room in the company of a horrible nurse who had no patience with me. She actually said that I had waited too long to have this baby (implying that I was old ... I was 27), and I told her I had just gotten married and couldn't have had the baby any sooner. In any event, I got through this episode and I will always remember that Jim was positively thrilled to see his new son, and to see me alive and quite happy. He left for work, but when he returned in the evening he was shocked by how sick I was. It seems that I had developed a "spinal headache" and could not lift my head. This was the result of careless nursing. The nurse had me sit up to change my hospital shirt, and she should have known better that people who have had an epidural should not sit up for several hours after receiving it, or they would have a "spinal headache." For five days, I laid in my bed not able to move. Jimmy was taken care of all that time by the nurses in the hospital. Finally, I was allowed to leave the hospital, heavily sedated for my headache, and Jim and I went home with our new baby.

It was a very difficult time for us because we had no one to help us, and we had to take care of this new baby. As I had never fed Jimmy in the hospital, I had to learn how to do this without anyone to guide me. Jim was a great help, as he had seen his sisters take care of their children. I, on the other hand, had never cared for a baby, and having this major headache wasn't helping. We survived for three days and nights, and thank God, Jimmy was a great baby. All he did was eat and sleep. After about three days, my mother flew to Cincinnati which was very brave of her, and when she arrived at our house, before she even took her hat off (she always wore a hat), she was giving the baby a bath. She couldn't believe that we had this baby home for three days and hadn't given him a bath. My mother stayed with us for ten days, and she was a Godsend. She taught me how to take care of the baby, and when she left, I was confident that I could do it.

In those days, most babies were fed by formula in a bottle. These bottles had to be sterilized every day.

One weekend, Jim and I were so tired that we decided to sterilize the bottles while we were sleeping. We set the alarm clock to go off in thirty minutes, but we never heard it. We finally woke up at about four in the morning to find the house was full of smoke and that the sterilizer had exploded and all the bottles broke and the nipples were stuck to the ceiling of the kitchen. We were in a panic. I grabbed Jimmy out of his crib and held him by an open window so he could breathe while Jim opened up the rest of the windows to let the smoke out. When we finally cleared the air, we were faced with a new dilemma … no sterilized bottles or nipples. Since it was 4 a.m., it was going to be hard to find more bottles, and at 6 a.m. Jimmy would want a bottle. Jim got in the car and found an all-night drug store where he proceeded to buy more bottles, nipples and a sterilizer kit. In those days, an all night drug store was very rare, but Jim knew I would have a nervous breakdown if the baby didn't have his bottle on time. This baby was on a schedule, and we never deviated from the schedule.

Eventually, we met other people, all of whom had moved to Cincinnati from the New York area. We had a lot in common, particularly the fact that we were all Catholics. We all had children or were about to have children so we were all in the same boat … away from home.

On weekends, we socialized at each other's homes. Mostly these were dinner parties where we got all dressed up and went out for drinks and dinner. We tried always to do something fun on the weekends because all week we gals stayed home, took care of our children and our husbands. On the weekends we were ready to go out, and we did.

Life in Cincinnati was just fun. It was such a clean city, and the people were really civilized. Then, Jim was transferred to Cleveland. I remember that professional movers came to our house and wrapped up everything in paper including Jim's shoes which he was planning to wear to Easter Sunday Mass. He wasn't too happy about that. I guess I could say we hated Cleveland. We moved there on the Monday after Easter. When we left Cincinnati, the sun was shining; when we got to Cleveland, it was a blizzard, which continued for several days. We lived in the back of a new apartment complex, and I remember thinking, "I wonder how Jim will get to work in this snow," but when he walked to the road in front of the building, the street was totally cleared off. Cleveland was a city that knew how to deal with snow removal; I was always impressed by that.

Our second son, Phillip, was born in Cleveland. I remember that Jim dropped me off at the front door of the hospital while he went to park the car. A nurse ran out of the hospital and asked me if I was in labor which was very obvious to her. She immediately put me in a wheelchair, raced me into the hospital, and by the time Jim returned, Phillip was about to be born. When I found out that Phillip was a redheaded baby, the only one in the hospital, I was thrilled. I always wanted a redheaded son. Jim named Phillip while I was kind of foggy from the anesthesia, and he spelled his name wrong. Jim was not a great speller. Anyway, "Phillip" with two "l's," rather than one "l," gave him distinction, and I was happy with it.

When I got back from the hospital, my mother had arrived and was taking care of Jimmy, thank God. It was the first time that Jimmy walked on his own; he was so happy to see me that he just let go of whatever he was holding on to and walked across the table into my arms.

After staying with me for about three days, my mother had to return to Brooklyn because my father was very ill. Sadly, my Dad died on October 31, 1964 at the age of 65, when Phillip was only twelve days old. It was Halloween night when my brother, Joseph, called to tell me that my father had died. It was a devastating phone call. I loved my father; he was always so kind and good to me. I think of him often; he has always been a major part of my life.

Now, Jim and I had to make plans to travel with two babies to New York. The first thing we had to do was get Phillip baptized. We would not travel anywhere with a new born baby not baptized. When Jim went to church to arrange the baptism, first explaining to the priest the unusual circumstance of my father's death and the need for us to travel to New York, the priest told Jim he could not baptize the baby without following all the proper procedures for the baptism, and that would take a few days. Jim, a person who would never disagree with a priest, told the priest that either he baptize the baby immediately, or we would baptize him ourselves, as we were not taking him on the plane without being baptized.

My son, Phillip, always says he started out his life in controversy and it stamped him forever.

When we got home to Brooklyn, we left Phillip with Jim's sister, Clare, who took great care of him while we handled the funeral. It was not good for a little baby, like Phillip, to be snatched from his mother at the age of two weeks, but there was nothing we could do about it. I was in a state of exhaustion, having just had a baby, and having another baby, Jimmy, who was thirteen months old, and barely able to walk.

After the funeral, I, and the two babies, stayed in Brooklyn, as my mother became very ill and had to have surgery on her eye. It was a wild time. Little Jimmy got pneumonia and had to be put in the hospital, as the doctor, the wonderful Dr. Jennings, who came to my mother's apartment immediately saw that I was suffering from exhaustion, and was not capable of nursing Jimmy properly. So off Jimmy went to the hospital at the age of fifteen months. He was such a great baby. He never carried on, and the nurses loved him. One day I went to the hospital to see him, and he wasn't in his bed. I was shocked and asked the nurse where he was. She said he was watching television. I said, "All by himself?" I rushed to the TV room, and there he was sitting there watching TV. The nurse had no idea he was so young. She said she thought he was two, and that's why they left him there watching the TV. Thank God, Jim recovered very quickly, and we brought him home.

We stayed in Brooklyn until the New Year, and then we returned to Cleveland. It was a difficult winter in Cleveland, as I think it always is. Jim traveled on the road for his business. He left every Monday and returned on Friday. I was alone with these two babies, and no support system, for five days every week. It was a very stressful time for me. I prayed that the two babies would not start crying at the same time, and thank God, that never happened. My whole life consisted of taking care of two babies all by myself.

With Jimmy in Cleveland

With Phillip in Cleveland

It Only Happens Now and Then ...

One episode I particularly remember was the day that Phillip, who was about four months old, became very ill. I had to get him to the doctor, so I put Jimmy in bed for his afternoon nap. Without fail, Jimmy always took a two to three hour nap. I asked my neighbor in the adjoining apartment to listen for him if he cried, but I was pretty sure he wouldn't wake up, as he just was so dependable, and if he did wake up, I had put some little books in his crib, and he would look at them until I returned.

I called a taxi and left for the doctor's office which was about five blocks from my house. When I got to the office, I had to wait a little while to see the doctor, and during the waiting time, it started to snow. When it snows in Cleveland, it's like nothing you have ever seen. It seems to immediately turn into a blizzard. Naturally, when I was finished with the doctor, it was impossible to get a cab. So there I was, with a sick baby, standing in the lobby of this medical building, wondering how I was going to get home, and what was going to happen to Jimmy all alone in the apartment. Then, I saw my milkman walking through the lobby. I explained my plight to him, and he said he would take me home. Phillip and I rode home in the cab of a milk truck. I thought to myself, there is something wrong with my situation here. It is too stressful, and I will never survive.

Early one morning we had quite a shock. Unbeknownst to us, Jimmy had gone off with his new found walking skills to seek adventure in the wide world. While were still asleep, he got out of his crib, opened the door of the apartment and walked down a busy road to watch construction men operate their machinery. One of the men saw him in his yellow pajamas, and wondered where he came from. He thought the child must have come from the apartment complex where we lived and brought him to the superintendent who of course recognized Jimmy. When he rang our bell and woke us up, we were shocked and horrified that Jimmy was out walking around the roads. We immediately had a bolt mounted at the top of the door so that this could never happen again. We felt it was like a miracle that he wasn't killed or kidnapped.

In the spring of that year, or perhaps it was the summer, we returned to Brooklyn to visit my mother, and when Jim went back to work, I stayed on with my mother and we went to the country house for a couple of weeks. We were supposed to stay for the summer, but I missed Jim, and the conditions in the country house were not favorable for taking care of two babies. So one morning my Mom and I decided to leave New Paltz and drive nine hours to Cleveland. We got on the Thruway and drove straight through to Cleveland. When we arrived there, I remember that Jim was sitting in the living room reading the paper. He was so surprised to see us, but he was glad. My mother gave me my Dad's new car to keep. She worried about me because when Jim traveled on the road all week, I was home in Cleveland without a car.

Having a car of my own made a great difference in my life. I was no longer isolated in the apartment complex with people with whom I had nothing in common.

It was while living in Cleveland that I developed a serious foot problem that was causing me great trouble. Because I was on my feet all day, taking care of two babies by myself most of the time while Jim was away traveling with his job, something happened to the arches of my feet. It was so bad that if the phone rang and I was not in the room with the phone, it would take about fifteen rings for me to answer it. This became a serious problem in taking care of the children, so I finally went to an orthopedic doctor who prescribed orthopedic shoes for me (I hated the shoes). These shoes were what we called "oxfords"; they laced up the front, and they had a steel shank to secure the arch of the foot. They did the job, and I really didn't care that I looked like an old lady as long as I could walk. I put these shoes on first thing in the morning and never took them off until bedtime. I had to laugh at what had happened to the frivolous person I once was who had an amazing collection of totally frivolous pointy-toed three inch heels. Now I was running around in these horrible brown suede oxfords, but at least I could run around. I guess this was the price I paid for all those years running around New York City in my three-inch heels.

Jimmy and Phillip in the country in the 1960s after we moved back to Brooklyn and bought a VW Beetle.

It Only Happens Now and Then …

We stayed in Cleveland until spring of the following year when Jimmy was 2 1/2 and Phillip was 1 1/2. I remember exactly the day that Jim decided to return to Brooklyn. It was St. Patrick's Day. We had called my mother to wish her a happy St. Patrick's Day, but she was very sad. She was all alone in Brooklyn, as my brother Tom lived in Massachusetts and my brother, Joseph, was in some other state traveling with the Army.

I was trying to console my mother when Jim said, "Tell your mother we are coming home." I looked at Jim and said, "Are we going on vacation?" He said, "No, we are leaving Cleveland and returning to Brooklyn." Just like that, he made up his mind. When I told my mother, she was so happy, and the die was cast. Later when I talked to Jim about this decision, he said he was actually not happy traveling on the road, he missed me and the children, and he thought it was ridiculous that my mother should be all alone in Brooklyn. In addition to all that, he had been thinking that he wanted to finish getting his degree from Brooklyn College. He said it would be good for the children to have a father who was a college graduate.

When Jim told his boss that he was leaving, his boss was very upset. The company that Jim worked for offered him a transfer to the Chicago territory, but Jim's mind was made up. He said there was a certain quality of life that he wanted with me and the children, and that did not include traveling on the road four nights a week. Jim gave the firm the required notice, and then made plans to go back to Brooklyn. One of the first things we did was to sell Jim's Dodge (we would replace it with a blue Volkswagen bug which we thought would be a good car to have in Brooklyn where parking was at a premium).

Jim then drove my car back to Brooklyn and lived with my mother for two weeks while he went about getting a new job and a place to live for our family. He had offers in the towel business, but they all entailed traveling and not living in New York. He was not interested in those. He took a job with the Wallace Pencil Company, and then concentrated on finding a house for us.

I always say that God took care of us because as soon as he started to look for a place to live, a house was vacated on the street where his sister lived. Normally, these houses are sold, but this time, the owner wanted to rent it. Jim immediately signed the lease and then he flew back to Cleveland to make arrangements for the move.

I must add here that while in Brooklyn with my mother, Jim gained 10 lbs. He said my mother took such good care of him and that he ate four meals a day. One of the four meals he always had in Brooklyn was probably a ham sandwich with mustard on pumpernickel bread. This was the favorite sandwich in our house, and since there were such great bakeries around the neighborhood, fresh pumpernickel was always on the table in our house. My mother couldn't do enough for Jim because he was returning to Brooklyn with me and the children. My mother never forgot that act of kindness on Jim's part, and that was what it was, a true act of kindness.

We called in the Mayflower moving company, and prepared for the move. It was very expensive, but my mother insisted that she would pay the moving costs which was extremely generous of her, and was much appreciated.

It took us two days to drive to Brooklyn, but we were happy to be going home. I think we were actually homesick. When we got to Brooklyn, I have to say that I was surprised at how much litter there was in the streets, and this was a little upsetting. Living on the "mean streets of Brooklyn" meant one had to adjust to clutter, cars all over, people all over and litter. But once you settle in a neighborhood and meet your neighbors and renew acquaintances with old friends, you adjust and in a short time, it's "home."

We lived in an attached house there, and it was quite small, about half the size of our future house in Montclair. There was a porch, a living room and a dining room and a kitchen on the first floor. Upstairs there were three bedrooms and a bathroom. And of course, it had a basement.

I have a classic story about the "basement" which was dark and dingy. I only went down there to do the laundry. One night I went out to play bridge with some friends. When we played bridge, we usually played for an hour and we chatted for three hours and so by the time we got home it was around midnight. When I was leaving to go out, Jim said to me, "Don't be too late, as you know I can't sleep until you are in." As it turns out, I was dropped off at the house around 12:30, but I couldn't get in the house as all the doors were locked. I rang the bell, banged on the doors, but Jim never heard me. I went next door and asked my neighbor if I could use the phone. I rang the phone countless times, but no one answered.

What was I to do? I couldn't stay in my neighbor's house all night so I went to the back door of my house and was able to access the basement. I couldn't get into the house itself as the kitchen door was bolted.

Did I mention that I was wearing a beautiful brand new outfit which consisted of a green dress and a matching coat? It was quite smashing. When I turned on the light in the basement, all these gigantic water bugs were crawling around … ugh … I was horrified. I had never been in the basement at night to witness this scene. I was exhausted and didn't know what to do. But as it turned out, we had boxes of beach towels from Jim's towel business so I took them out of the boxes and put them on top of the washer and dryer and climbed up there and if you can believe it, I went to sleep.

When I woke up it was dawn and the milkman was coming down the driveway. I jumped up because I didn't want him to look in the window of the basement and think there was the body of a fully clothed woman lying on top of the washer and dryer. I ran upstairs to the kitchen and began banging on the kitchen door. When Jim finally opened the door, he said, "Where have you been all night?"

I looked at him like he was crazy. I said, "Where do you think I've been?"

He said, "I thought maybe you decided to stay over at your girlfriend's."

I stared at him incredulously and said, "Have you ever known me to stay out all night?" and a few other "choice" words. I told him that for a man "who couldn't sleep unless I was home," he didn't have any trouble that night. I could have been dead in the alley between the houses and he would have never known. He told me that Jimmy had awakened him in the middle of the night to ask, "Where was Mommy?" and he had said, "She probably stayed over at a friend's house."

I was really mad, and I told Jim I was going to bed and that he should take a day off and take care of the children, and he did. He knew he was in trouble this time.

I was happy to return to Brooklyn. I think I missed it more than I thought I did. I missed my mother, my Aunt Peggy and my Uncle Chris and all my wonderful friends who have remained my friends through all these years. There are no friends like old friends.

Jim enrolled in Brooklyn College again, and he went to college four nights a week from 6 to 10:45 p.m. He seemed to do this effortlessly and I took care of the children. By this time, we were expecting our third child, and my mother was a great help to us. She was so glad to have us back.

In June of 1966, Jim graduated from Brooklyn College, and it was a great feat. He had put a lot of time and effort into this degree. During the previous summer, he took thirteen credits, as he was anxious the get finished with college. We had planned a great party to mark the occasion and had invited Jim's family and my family. The invitations were out, the food was ordered and everyone was looking forward to the great celebration, and then Robert F. Kennedy was killed. The whole country was in mourning. We were in a quandary as to what to do. A lot of effort had gone into Jim's getting the degree, and he deserved some recognition. Our phone began to ring. "Was the party on?" Our answer to everyone who called was, "If Jim died, and RFK was having a big party to celebrate a great occasion, would he cancel the party?" Everyone got the message, and the party went forward, and it was a great celebration.

Jim graduated right before Stephen was born. It was record hot weather in Brooklyn, and we had no air conditioning. Our backyard was so hot that the day before Stephen was born on July 7th, 1966, it was 108 degrees in the yard. That's because the sun was beating down on the concrete that covered this city yard. I have to mention here that I was suffering from a severe case of poison oak and had blisters about the size of a 50 cent piece all over my legs. When I told the obstetrician about this, he didn't seem to be concerned, but when I arrived at the hospital to have Stephen, all the staff went crazy when they saw me. They immediately wrapped my legs in bandages, terrified that I would contaminate the hospital. I had warned them, but they didn't listen. Anyway, Stephen was born in the midst of all this commotion about the poison oak, and the result of this is that Stephen is impervious to poison ivy or poison oak. He can literally sit in a field of poison oak, and it wouldn't affect him. As a matter of fact, and to prove this point, on July 4th, 1976, the Bicentennial, our family went to view the procession of the tall ships from a park near the George Washington Bridge, and we all got a severe case of poison ivy, except Stephen, who has a natural immunity to it as a result of the circumstances of his birth.

Did I mention that the hospital where Stephen was born, the Peck Memorial Hospital, where I also was born, had no air conditioning? Those were the dark ages.

Now Jim and I had three beautiful sons, age 3 1/2 and under. It was a monumental job to take care of them, but my mother was wonderful. I thanked God we moved back to Brooklyn. For the first few months of Stephen's life, my mother would arrive at our house at around eleven in the evening and take over the care of Stephen so that I could get a full night's sleep. She gave him the eleven o'clock bottle and then took care of him through the night. My mother totally bonded with Stephen, and there was no doubt that he was her favorite grandchild. He was the first grandchild she got her hands on as all of her other grandchildren lived far away. She really loved him, and all the other boys always said that Stephen was Grandma's "favorite."

In the next year, Jimmy was preparing to go to kindergarten, and we were preparing for a new baby. I remember that in the summer months when I was heavily pregnant and taking care of three boys, I used to send Jimmy with some money to buy bread for the family. He had to walk to the corner and over a couple of blocks to get to the bread store. As a reward he had just enough money to buy himself a single Tootsie Roll with the change. When I look back on this, it's remarkable I felt safe sending a four year old onto the streets of Brooklyn and equally remarkable that he always accomplished the mission. Later when we moved to Montclair, walking to school was a piece of cake for Jimmy.

Mark was born in November of 1968. I remember that we brought Mark home the day before Thanksgiving, and on Thanksgiving, I cooked Thanksgiving dinner. I can't believe I did that, but I did, as Jim was really into Thanksgiving. It's his favorite holiday. Of course, Jim took care of the children, with the aid of Grandma, while I cooked the dinner.

It Only Happens Now and Then …

Moving to Montclair

In September of 1968, our landlord told us he wanted us to move as he desired to sell the house. At that time I was seven months pregnant, but we had to move and so we began to look for a house to buy. Because Jimmy was about to go to school, we wanted to settle some place with a good school system, and I didn't want to move again. We first went to Long Island to look because Jim's brother lived there, but after spending one Sunday on Long Island, in the traffic, we decided Long Island was not for us. We then set our eyes on New Jersey as we had friends there and we liked the idea that the traffic was better and the area seemed to be less crowded than Long Island.

We were looking in Nutley because my brother Tom once lived there and it was the only town we really knew about. Nothing appealed to us there, or in Teaneck, where we also looked. The houses seemed too small for us, and then we were driving home and we came into this town with all these great trees and I said to Jim, "What is the name of this place?" He said, "Montclair," and I said, "This is the town." I just fell in love with the trees. (I later found out there were 40,000 trees in Montclair.) We went to the first realtor we saw, and we were so fortunate to meet Mrs. Trewhella, who became our agent. She was a lovely woman, and we just related to her. She explained to us about the town. She was very proud of Montclair. She told us about the churches and schools, and promised us that she would not call us to see anything that didn't have what we wanted and was not in our price range.

One of the things that we definitely wanted was room for my mother. The houses in Montclair were very large and most of them had a third floor with a bathroom. This was something that definitely appealed to us as we didn't want to leave my mother in Brooklyn all by herself.

Our realtor understood exactly what we wanted, and on the third trip to Montclair, under Mrs. Trewhella's direction, we found the house. By this time, I was eight months pregnant, and in a state of high stress, as our landlord in Brooklyn really wanted to get rid of us. I had originally wanted to buy another house that she showed us, but Jim did not like the house. One reason was that it was on a corner and would require a lot of snow shoveling, and Jim wasn't "into" shoveling. Jim made the right decision there.

It seemed to me that we found the house fairly fast, but upon talking to Jim's sister, Mary, she said she could recall that we spent an enormous amount of time looking for the house and she remembered that the New York Times real estate section was always open on our coffee table in Brooklyn, as we searched and searched for the house.

I remember very well the day we saw the house. We had come to look at another house on the same block, and this was the house that Jim absolutely did not like. After Jim rejected this house, Mrs. Trewhella took us around the corner and drove into the block from another direction so that we did not realize we were on the same street. (The upper part of the block was not in good condition and this house was located on the lower part of the block.) Anyway, the house we were now going to see was a true center hall colonial which I always wanted, but we could not afford as the center hall colonial was always more expensive.

As soon as I stepped into this house, I loved it. It was a charming house and it had lots of space which is something my brother Tom told me to look for. He said the one thing we needed, with four growing boys, was "space." I immediately said before going through the house that it was great, but we couldn't afford it.

We had determined that we could spend $30,000 for a house, and that was it. Mrs. Trewhella convinced us to look through the house before we ruled it out. So we walked through it, and it was great. It had a lovely third floor with a bathroom which was perfect for my mother. I actually didn't look at the third floor because in my "delicate condition," I wasn't into walking up the stairs. Jim looked in the basement, although he knew nothing about basements and boilers, and said it looked good to him. The antique boiler remained functional for over forty more years. We looked at the backyard which was truly lovely, as the woman who owned the house never allowed her four boys to play on the lawn. It was like a golf course.

We never really looked at the garage. That is how casual we were about buying a house.

Mrs. Trewhella convinced us to make an offer. She said, "You never know." So we made an offer of $32,500 which was more than we could afford. The sellers rejected it, as they had already turned down an offer for $34,000. A couple of weeks later, Mrs. Trewhella called us and said they were willing to negotiate. The only thing we had to negotiate was the fact that we would waive the inspection. We figured that the people were living in the house, it was operating with a family living in it, and it would operate when they were gone.

As it was now October, and the sellers had already purchased a house, and there were no buyers on the horizon, they accepted the offer.

Since we had only seen the house once (in those days people usually looked at houses many times before they made a decision), Mrs. Bennett, the seller of the house, called me in Brooklyn to ask me if I would like to come out to see the house again, and measure for curtains, etc. I said, "No, the house was fine." She thought this was strange and actually worried that we were not seriously interested. To tell the truth, with three little boys to take care of, and with my being about to deliver our fourth child, I was not in physical condition to make a trip out to Montclair and measure for curtains.

The closing on the house was scheduled for December 13th, a Friday, and since I am my mother's daughter, I would not close on Friday the 13th. We closed on the 12th of December, 1968, and we moved into the house on the 14th of December. Before all this came to pass, we had Mark on the 20th of November, we celebrated Thanksgiving in Brooklyn and we packed up for the move to New Jersey. In the midst of all this chaos, I decided that I would color my hair red. Jim always considered me a redhead, but I was really auburn haired, and I decided to "reinvent" myself and move into Montclair as a redhead. I already had two redheaded little boys, and so, everyone in Montclair thought I was a true redhead, and so to this day I am described by people who know me in Montclair as that "redheaded Mary Hamilton."

December of 1968 was a particularly snowy month and the weather conditions were not good for moving. On the day of the closing we drove to the house with Jim's nephew, William, who shoveled the walk so that we could get into the house. We actually got lost trying to find Gordonhurst Avenue. We brought with us that night our good china and our Waterford crystal because we didn't want the movers to handle these precious things.

The next day, bright and early, the movers were at the house in Brooklyn. It was a cold, freezing day.

We left our new baby with Aunt Mary and prepared for our journey to New Jersey with the three boys.

Phillip recalls that we just told the children, "We are moving today to New Jersey." He said it was not a big deal and there was no psychological preparation for the children to deal with the move. It was "just the way it was." It took a long time to pack up the house. In the meantime, Stephen was sick and throwing up in a bucket in the living room. When everything was on the truck, we put the three children in the car and drove to Montclair. When we arrived in Montclair it was very cold and there was about two feet of snow on the ground. All the doors of the house were open, and the heat was pumping like crazy, and all I could think of was all the money for heating the house was going out the door.

Jim just pitched in to help the moving men. He worked so hard, and I particularly remember him carrying in the toy chest which was full of toys and was extremely heavy. I thought he would have a heart attack, but he was young and strong and determined to get this thing done so that we could shut the doors and keep the heat in the house. In the meantime, Jimmy and Phillip were having a great time exploring the house, and Stephen was still throwing up in a bucket in the living room. I can remember standing in the kitchen exhausted (you have to remember I just had a baby), and my new neighbor, Eveline Köchling, came in the back door with a thermos of tea. I was so happy to see her, and I told her that moving was such a traumatic experience that I would never do it again.

But she said, "Of course you will." I ended up living in this house for over 40 years, and I truly loved it.

On the day we moved in, Eveline's two boys, Heinz and Eddy, were outside in their Wellingtons throwing snowballs at their front door. They were not the least bit destructive; they simply had inherited a great scientific curiosity from their father and they were testing to see if their new Plexiglas window was really unbreakable. This was typical of the Köchling boys, and they immediately asked Jimmy and Phillip to join in the fun.

The boys all became great friends over the years, and Jim and I feel blessed that we lived among such fine people. Dr. Köchling was German and Eveline was Irish. Joe Köchling was a Chemist with a PhD from MIT. Our neighbors on the other side were John and Pauline Davis and their three children. Dr. Davis was a PhD from Brown University, and across the street was George White who had a degree from MIT. We were surrounded by these highly intellectual people, and Jim used to say that they probably thought "there goes the neighborhood" when we moved in. Nevertheless, we all got along, and it was a great neighborhood for our sons to live in. We all had different beliefs but we shared the same values so it was easy to raise children in a disciplined way.

Now … back to moving day. When the movers were finally finished, I remember that we all went to the Red Chimney restaurant on Route 3 and had supper. We were exhausted beyond belief. My foot was hurting so bad that it was actually bleeding. The next day, Sunday, we got up early, went to Mass at our new parish, St. Cassian's, and proceeded to go to Brooklyn to pick up Mark and bring him home.

Monday, it was "business as usual" as Jim went back to work in the city. I went to work taking care of four little boys (including a three week old baby Mark), and trying to make some order out of the chaos of moving. I can remember that I was so happy to be in this house. I loved it from the first moment, and I truly felt that I was home and that this was where I belonged. I had a lot to do as Christmas was approaching, and we were not ready.

We decided not to send Jimmy to kindergarten as it was just not convenient at this time. It would be impossible to get him to school and take care of the other children. Jim would be traveling to New York early in the morning, and there was no one to watch the children while I walked Jimmy to school, so he stayed home. Actually, it was like the experience of being in kindergarten right in our house. The children were very bright, and they managed to play all day either together or by themselves, and I managed to keep busy, as you can imagine, just taking care of the four children.

The next weekend, my mother made the trip from Brooklyn to visit us. She came all by herself from the Port of Authority and she walked down Gordonhurst. When she got to the house, she came in the front door and immediately she loved the house. We took her on a tour and showed her the room on the third floor, and when she came down, she said that she was very happy that there was room in this house for her. I think she was not sure what type of house it was, and she was so pleased that it was so big and roomy. After that, my mother came every weekend, and she was an enormous help to us.

I will try now to write things down as I remember them at that time. The first thing I vividly remember is that it was snowing when we moved in and it kept snowing until late

March of that year. I had never seen such snow. The boys loved it and were outside playing all day. I was outside shoveling. I asked my neighbor if it was usual for it to snow like this, as it never snowed in Brooklyn like this, and she said Montclair was west of the city and in a snow belt. I didn't know that, but it sure seemed that way to me. Every day, I dressed the baby up very warm and put him in his carriage on the enclosed porch, and then I went out to play with the children, or do my jobs around the house. Mark spent the first six months of his life practically in the outdoors. The porch was a Godsend. If it was really too cold to play outside, I dressed the boys warmly, and they played on the porch for a good part of the day. It was like a big outdoor playpen. They were safe and they were outside which was good for me.

Christmas was fast approaching and we didn't have any presents for the children from Santa. The next weekend my mother came, and Jim and I went shopping to Two Guys (a discount department store someone had told us about) to find toys for the children. It was almost Christmas Eve; it was snowing, and we were desperate to get the presents. We had a hard time finding the store, and when we did, we got two shopping carts and ran around the store picking up the presents. When we had filled the two carts, we left the store and were much relieved that we had accomplished our mission. Christmas was very important to us, especially Jim. He was so enthusiastic about Christmas, and his enthusiasm was infectious. When we finally got home, in a blinding snowstorm, Jim dragged all the presents into the basement and hid them. There was no sign of Christmas in our house.

On Christmas Eve, when the children were asleep, Jim and I set about turning our house into a "Christmas House." We had an artificial tree so Jim went down to the basement and brought up the tree which for some reason I put together. All the lights and decorations were put on it, and the house was decorated. It took hours to do this. All the presents were put under the tree, and we went to bed about 4 a.m. When the children woke up, and came downstairs the whole house was "Christmas" and the children were so surprised. It was great fun to watch them wonder at what had happened in the middle of the night.

We carried on with this game for about four years, and then we physically could not do it anymore as it was exhausting. My mother used to watch us, and she thought we were crazy to wait until the last minute like we did, but she never went to bed until it was all done.

Jim and I put a lot of thought into the presents we gave the children. We tried to always give them things to stimulate their imagination. They played for hours with their toys, and Jim devoted all Christmas day to playing with the boys while I cooked the turkey. Jim would lie on the floor and play soldiers and build with the wooden blocks the boys got one year. The blocks were the best gift I think. It was a huge box of blocks that we bought from a school supplier. The boys would build things like skyscrapers, and the buildings would be higher than they were. When they were building these structures, they wore yellow hats like construction workers, so that if the buildings fell down, which they inevitably did, they wouldn't hurt their heads. These blocks made great forts for their soldiers, and also cities where they would put their Fisher Price little wooden people. I think the blocks were to them what Lego is to the children of this generation. We still have these blocks and our grandchildren are now playing with them.

Since the living room was so big, the children would make their "set-ups" with the blocks in there, and many times, the set-up would stay for days and they were a work in progress. After all the children's work to make the setup, I just couldn't take it down when they went to bed. Rather I would leave it there, and they would come down in the morning and start working on it all over again. This could go on for several days, but as the weekend approached, Jim wanted to live like a "civilized" man, and he would put all the blocks away, at least for Saturday night, and as I recall, on Sunday afternoon, the serious business of playing started all over again. I loved watching the children play. They seemed so intelligent to me, and they were never bored.

Jim always took the week between Christmas and New Year's as a vacation week. He played with the children all week. When they were older, he particularly spent a lot of time reading the directions of board games and playing with the boys.

I remember the first New Year's Eve we spent in the house. Our friend, Betty, had come to visit us and stayed overnight. It was a quiet night. The three of us drank champagne and sat and looked at the fire.

A fireplace was a great novelty to us, and we all loved it. My mother taught us how to make a proper fire based on her years of experience in Ireland.

After New Year's, I sprang into action and decided to start painting the house which was no easy task, but I was determined. For some reason, the cabinets in the kitchen were painted red ... it was horrible, and I immediately proceeded to turn them into my favorite color, teal. I ordered the paint from a firm in New England which specialized in colonial colors. Since I couldn't leave the house to do any shopping, everything had to be ordered via mail. That worked great for me. If I wanted something, I could just call and have it delivered. I think I painted the whole interior of the house without once having to go to the paint store or the hardware store. Montclair was a great town. At that time, you could just call up Thompson's Hardware and literally tell them you needed a paint brush and some sandpaper and they would deliver it to you that day. That would never happen in Brooklyn.

So while the children played, either in the living room or on the porch, I would paint. I had a regular schedule for painting. I painted every morning from 10 until 12:30. After that, I put the paint away, made lunch for the boys, put the two youngest in for naps, then went down and made dinner because at five o'clock I was too tired to make dinner. In the meantime, most of my afternoon was spent doing laundry, although I must admit that from 2:30 to 3:00, I took time out to watch a soap opera which I had been watching since Jimmy was born. I don't know how I got hooked on this soap opera, but I did. As a matter of fact, I even got my mother hooked on it, and she never watched daytime TV. When I went to the hospital to give birth to Stephen, I asked my mother to watch the program and tell me what happened because it was, or at least I thought it was, a crucial time in the story. Of course, as usual, nothing happened, but by that time, my mother was hooked on the soap opera. My mother and I watched this soap opera for about two more years, and then one day, it was so stupid, that we both decided to get up and shut off the TV and never watch it again. Later on, we would talk about how foolish we were to waste our precious time like that.

Of course, when I was painting, I never realized how bad this was for a new baby. One day, Mark, who was about three months old when all this painting was going on, started to wheeze and couldn't breathe. This was the first time, since I moved to Montclair, that I needed to get a doctor. It will seem strange to anyone reading this to believe that we lived in Montclair for at least three months without getting a pediatrician for four young children, but we had our wonderful Dr. Jennings, in Brooklyn, who was about 80 years old at the time, and had taken care of our children up to this time. Whenever the children or the baby, Mark, needed to have shots, we always made a trip to Brooklyn. It was a 45 minute drive from our house in Montclair, and from what people were telling me, often the wait to see a doctor in Montclair was two hours. We talked it over with Dr. Jennings and he said to just continue with him for the time being. So, this one day when Mark started to wheeze and couldn't breathe, as a result of my painting, I put him in the car with all the other children and drove to Brooklyn. I went through the Lincoln Tunnel, down the West Side Highway in New York, through the Battery Tunnel, and finally arrived at Dr. Jennings office on Midwood Street in Brooklyn.

He lived in an old brownstone house, with his spinster sister, who took care of him. When she saw all of us at the front door, she wasn't too happy, but fortunately, the boys were well behaved. If they weren't, they would hear from Miss Jennings. She would give them a "look" that would control them. If ever the boys would think of misbehaving, just being in this very old and very beautiful brownstone would stop them. From the minute the lace curtained front door opened and we were ushered into a formal parlor by Miss Jennings, to the moment Dr. Jennings opened the oak pocket door of his office and stood there in his white coat looking at the children, they seemed to be tranquilized. His very appearance was enough to command the utmost respect. He was a tall, thin man with aquiline features, and he wore little silver rimmed glasses down on his nose. The way Dr. Jennings worked was that he gave you an appointment, and there was never anyone waiting in his waiting room. I think he believed that sick children didn't need to interact with each other. He took Mark into his office, and proceeded to give him a shot of adrenalin … he was that bad. He then lectured me on my stupidity of painting while there was an infant in the house. Of course, he was right.

Here in my story, I am going to make a digression to tell you a little bit more about Dr. Jennings. When we met him he was about 80 years old. He had been the head of pediatrics at Kings County Hospital (similar to Bellevue in New York) in Brooklyn for many years and was semi-retired.

Dr. Jennings was a wonderful man. Everyone in Brooklyn knew of his reputation and, of course, at his age, he did not take any new patients. He took us because he had known the Hamilton family for years, and we first came to see him, when we brought Jimmy to him because Jimmy had been born with a hemangioma on his left temple, and Jim's sister, Clare, was very concerned about it. She called Dr. Jennings and asked him to look at it for us. That is how we became his patients, or at least our children did. I think he was very interested in young

Jimmy, and he decided to keep an eye on him. He sent us to Sloan Kettering in New York for further evaluations, but after a couple of years of going there, once a year for a checkup, Dr. Jennings decided it wasn't anything serious. He assured me that by the time Jimmy was 21, it would be gone, and it was.

Because Dr. Jennings was such an unusual man, I would like to share a couple of Dr. Jennings stories.

He was a man of a few words, so I was really surprised one afternoon when he began to just chat with me. In the course of the conversation, I asked him what the most unusual thing he had ever seen was. He proceeded to tell me how he had taken care of one particularly prominent family in Brooklyn through several generations and saw all the children of this family. The original family had one daughter who had never married, and Dr. Jennings referred to her as a "typical spinster." He said she was an unusual child, and he always remembered her as being a "strange little girl" with all sorts of allergies. About thirty years later, a little girl belonging to this same large family became his patient, and he said it was extraordinary how much she was like her great aunt whom he had treated so long ago. She looked exactly like her and had all her mannerisms and allergies. The aunt was deceased and the child never knew her, but he did, and he saw the aunt in this child. He said the gene pool was a fascinating thing, and because he had been a pediatrician so long taking care of the same family for years, he was able to witness the phenomenon of how genes are passed on.

On another visit to his office, we had to wait because he was late. That was very unusual for Dr. Jennings, and he explained to me the reason for his tardiness. He said he had been asked to come to Kings County Hospital for a

196

consultation regarding something that the doctors there were unable to identify. He said he walked into the ward, looked at the child, and immediately told the young doctors that the child had scarlet fever. They had never actually seen a case of scarlet fever. They had read about it, but had never seen it because rarely in the sixties did anyone ever get scarlet fever. Dr. Jennings told me that in his time he had seen so much scarlet fever, "I could smell it."

On another occasion, when I told Dr. Jennings that the most popular pediatrician in Montclair had his office right around the corner from my home, and his name was Dr. Waldron, Dr. Jennings told me he had trained Dr. Waldron at Kings County. He also told me he saw no need for me to change doctors, as most childhood problems could be handled with a yearly visit. He said he would prescribe, as necessary, over the phone, as the new antibiotics could take care of most childhood illnesses. And he was right. We never had to rush our children to the hospital for anything, thank God. If ever anything seemed amiss with them, I called him, described their condition, answered his questions, and then he made a diagnosis. He was a genius. And no matter what time I called him, he always answered the phone himself on the first ring. I remember the only time I called him in a panic was when Jimmy was about three years old, and woke up in the middle of the night wheezing. Jim and I thought he was dying. It was the only time Jim called a doctor for one of the children. Dr. Jennings immediately answered the phone; Jim described the situation and Dr. Jennings told us to bring Jimmy to the phone so he could hear him breath. After listening a while, he told us he was having an asthma attack, that it was not fatal in a child his age, and to put him in the bathroom with the shower running to create steam. We did that and he was fine. This was our first experience with asthma, but we learned to stay calm, as Dr. Jennings told us. As it turned out, all of our children were prone to attacks like that, but with the medication Dr. Jennings prescribed, we got through childhood without any major trauma.

Here I have to mention Dr. Jennings' fee. He charged $5.00 for a visit to his office, and one day he told me he was going to raise his fee to $7.00. Compared to what it was costing in Montclair to go to a doctor, this was ridiculously low. When I went to him the next time, I was making out my check and he said to "make it $5.00." He said, "I changed my mind." I think he was just such a generous man and he felt the trip from Montclair to Brooklyn was expensive enough. In any case, he was "one in a million."

Another Dr. Jennings story that comes to mind was the time Jimmy, about ten years old at the time, came home from school with a rash on his neck. It was about the size of a fifty cent piece and formed a perfect circle. I looked at it and immediately called Dr. Jennings and described the situation to him. He immediately said, "He has a shingle." He asked me if Jimmy had had the chicken pox before we became his patient, and Jimmy did have the chicken pox when he was three months old and we lived in Cincinnati. Dr. Jennings said the shingle was the result of his being exposed to someone having the chicken pox. He said Jimmy would not get the chicken pox again, but that the other boys would have the chickenpox in ten days because they were exposed to it. I actually couldn't believe this, but sure enough, ten days later Phillip, Stephen and Mark had the chickenpox.

The last time I saw Dr. Jennings was in 1980 when Jimmy was preparing to go to West Point. West Point needed a medical history on Jimmy, and the only doctor who had ever really seen him was Dr. Jennings, so we made one last trip to Brooklyn to see him. He was very pleased that Jimmy was going to go to West Point and felt he would do well there. Shortly after that trip, Dr. Jennings died. Although Dr. Jennings was a life-long bachelor with no children of his own, there were countless mothers in Brooklyn who named one of their sons "Kenneth" in honor of him.

The problem with digressions is that it is hard to get back into the story, but here goes...

When I finished painting the living room, dining room and kitchen, it was fast approaching my favorite holiday, St. Patrick's Day, and Jim and I decided to have a housewarming/St. Patrick's Day Party.

The one thing that Jim and I always had was enthusiasm. Everything we got into, we got into with a vengeance. St. Patrick's Day was always a great day for us. We even got engaged on St. Patrick's Day.

Planning a big party, in a big house, was such fun. Jim and I spent hours discussing who we would invite, what we would serve, and what music we would play. We put a lot of effort into any entertaining that we ever did.

Even though the children were very young, they caught the excitement in the air as we prepared for the party. We sent out invitations, and told everyone to wear something green. My mother got caught up in the enthusiasm, and decided to make Jim and me matching green velvet vests with brass buttons to wear at the party. We had these vests for years, and many years after, our son, Phillip, took over the wearing of the vest.

We polished the floors so that we would be able to dance. This house had a great living room with a beautiful oak floor, and since there was no rug on it, it was the perfect place to do some Irish dancing. We had some great Irish records, and we decided we would play Irish music all night so that everyone would know this was a real Irish party. Part of the décor for the party was the fireplace and the ten brass candlesticks that were on the mantelpiece. These candlesticks were my mother's and my grandmother's and my mother had brought them from Ireland. Every year I made a major project of polishing them, and it was a labor of love. Every time I polished them, I felt a kinship with my mother and my grandmother, and I wondered what hands were around these candlesticks when they were used in Ireland for traveling around a house in the dark. It was almost a mystical experience for me. On the night of the party, I put green candles in them, and just before the guests arrived they were lit and the fireplace was set ablaze. It was instant decorating. It set the tone for the whole evening. Actually, sometimes it was too warm, but we lit them anyway.

The party was a massive undertaking on my part. Of course, Jim did a lot of work also. It was a big job just to maintain some sort of order with four little children in the house, and Jim was great at neatening things up.

 I made all the food, which consisted of all sorts of hors d'oeuvres, dips and Irish sandwiches of meat and bread. My father always made the most delicious sandwiches and they were made with a light coating of butter, plenty of great meat on good bread, cut in quarters. He said that was the way sandwiches were made in Ireland. These were good for parties because you could just pick them up in your hand and devour them. The men loved them, as they didn't have to hassle with the buffet line and the buffet plate. You could just pick up a drink and a sandwich and be on your way. Jim and I always thought that interrupting the party to sit down and eat took away from the spontaneity of the event

At this first of many St. Patrick's Day parties, we had all friends and relatives from Brooklyn, as we didn't yet know anyone in Montclair. The house was full, and everyone was very enthusiastic about the size of the house. We put the children to bed, but the noise level was so high that they woke up and sat on the stairs and watched the proceedings

We always said the party was a three-tier affair. First we had the cocktail party when the guests arrived and greeted one another; then we moved into the sandwich and beer phase where the serious dancing took place, and then we moved into the "soda bread" phase where we served coffee and Irish soda bread. My Aunt Peggy made the greatest soda bread, and she always arrived at the party with several loaves. Other people brought soda bread too, but no one could duplicate Aunt Peggy's. As a matter of fact, when all the soda bread was displayed on the table over the years, friends would come up to me and ask, "Which is Aunt Peggy's?" That was the one they wanted.

When I reminisce about those parties, I have to laugh because the "coffee phase" of this party consisted of "Irish coffee," and that does not sober one up for the drive home. It was very irresponsible of us to serve so much alcohol, but I guess that's what made the parties such fun. Thank God, no one was ever involved in an auto accident leaving the party.

Speaking of "leaving the party" reminds me of a story about the very first party. My friends Bobbie and Matty Parker were at the party, and it was about 2 a.m., and Matty wanted to leave. Bobby was having such a good time that she didn't want to leave, so Matty said, "I'm going," and with that he got in his car and drove off. Jim thought we were going to have Bobby all night, but fortunately Matty just drove around the block and came back for Bobby. Jim breathed a sigh of relief because Bobby was a non-stop talker and Jim didn't relish the idea of spending the next day listening to her and probably having to return her to Brooklyn.

The next year we added friends we met in Montclair to the guest list, and the party took on a life of its own. We had such great friends in Montclair. We loved them all. I think we met most of them at Marie and Bob McKeown's house over the Christmas holidays of our second year in Montclair. What a great group they were. Everyone had a marvelous joie de vie.

So when St. Patrick's Day arrived, we added about twelve people to the guest list. I can remember that the party ran the same way as the first one, but it was better because added to this party was an Irish bachelor who lived on the block. His name was Gene Byrne, and St. Patrick's Day was his favorite holiday also. He was totally booked up for St. Patrick's Day, but he put us down in his little black book (which he always carried to note social engagements), and sure enough, he arrived at our house at around 1 a.m. when the party was in full swing, or at least, I thought it was in full swing. Gene arrived with two other bachelors and they were all dressed in "tails" having come from some formal affair. Gene was the most marvelous dancer, and he began to waltz around the room with the ladies. Then he decided he would teach us how to do a great Irish dance called the "Siege of Ennis." It was what we call a "set" dance, and almost everyone got up on the floor while Gene instructed us in the machinations of the dance. Normally, the men wouldn't get up for this, but because they were "half in the bag," they were into it. Gene also taught us how to do the Highland Fling, another set dance, which everyone does together. We had so much fun with these dances that the party roared on until four in the morning. To this day, we are still doing these two dances at family parties and weddings.

Other neighbors, Brendan and Kathy Carney, who lived a few houses down from us on Gordonhurst were a great asset to the party. Brendan was a big, hulking Irishman, with an infectious smile, great wit, and a mane of prematurely grey hair. He loved to dance, but only Irish dances. He wasn't a great dancer, but his enthusiasm made up for his lack of dancing skill. His enthusiasm was so great and his foot stomping so vigorous that one night, I actually thought the floor would cave in. Of course, his wife, Kathy was a great dancer, and she made him look good. Kathy was more Irish than the Irish at these gatherings, though she never failed to express pride in her Slovakian ancestry. The first time they came to our party, Kathy, who was a great baker, made a huge green shamrock cake. They were absolutely great friends and spent every St. Patrick's Day and New Year's Eve with us for years. A funny story here is that for these parties, Jim always wore his tuxedo, and Brendan would always arrive in a plaid flannel shirt much to Kathy's chagrin.

Somewhere along the line, Brendan decided that he would dress up for the party, and everyone made a big thing of the fact that Brendan gave up his plaid shirt. Brendan was much loved by all. He was so intelligent and quick witted that everyone loved to banter with him. Sad to say, Brendan died suddenly one Memorial Day weekend, and Jim said "it was like a library burned down" because Brendan was a major historian and kept a treasure trove of historical knowledge in his brain which he shared with all who were interested.

The St. Patrick's Day party became an annual event at Hamilton House. It was held on the Saturday before St. Patrick's Day or on St. Patrick's Day, March 17th, if it fell on a Friday or Saturday.

We always made plans for getting to Sunday Mass, of course, and we went to the late Saturday Mass at five o'clock so we wouldn't have to get going too early on Sunday after staying up until 4 a.m. The kids loved the day after the party. It was a totally crazy day. Before we went to bed, we left snacks in the living room for the children so that they could eat something and not wake us up. This seemed like a good idea until the day when Stephen was running and sliding across the polished floor and put his hand up to stop and broke the front window. Needless to say, we never slept in again. No matter how tired we were, we dragged ourselves downstairs to keep an eye on the children. It could have been a tragedy, but thank God, only the window was damaged.

Life in Montclair in the 1970s was quite an old fashioned experience. Once Jim and I had our set of friends, we had a great social life. We went out almost every Saturday to either a dinner party or a dance. If you drove down any street in Montclair on a Saturday evening you would always see cars parked and one house on the block would be all lit up, and you could look in the windows of the house and see people milling around having cocktails. Those were the years of the cocktail party.

We all took turns entertaining, and, with our crowd, it was usually dinner parties. All the ladies worked hard all week taking care of their families, their houses, their husbands, and then on Saturday night, they were ready to go out. Our husbands understood us, and they didn't mind putting on a shirt and tie on Saturday night, and going out with us. They understood that the ladies needed to get away from the house and do some socializing. In those days, there were no DVD players, or videos, or home entertainment centers, and so people went out to socialize. Jim and I were particularly lucky in that my mother was always available to babysit for us.

Actually, Jim and I really made an effort to have something on the calendar for every weekend so that my mother would come from Brooklyn to help us. She just didn't want to come for no reason; but she was always happy to come if we needed her.

For a few years, we even traveled to Brooklyn on a Saturday night, but that all ended one night on our return to Montclair. We were driving on the West Side Highway in Manhattan on our way to the Lincoln Tunnel, and we were exiting the highway at 1 a.m. I was driving, and we were going down the off ramp, and coming up the down ramp was a car heading right at us. Fortunately, he saw us and stopped, and I stopped. It was such a shock to us that we decided when we got home that from now on all our socializing would be done in Montclair. Our children were so young, and we had to stay alive until they were grown because there was no one to take care of them in the event of our demise.

We were in the busy years of marriage. First of all, our son Jim was going into the first grade at the same time as Phillip was going into kindergarten. I had to drive Jimmy to school each morning as it was too far to walk, and I had to get Phillip to kindergarten in a different direction. I often left the two little children in the house while I ran around delivering the other children to their schools. Thank God, Stephen was such a good child that I could sit him in the living room, surround him with his soldiers and he would just play there until I returned. In the meantime, Mark would be sleeping or playing in his crib. This whole scenario took about twenty minutes. I was a nervous wreck leaving them in the house, but there really was nothing I could do. Fortunately, we had great neighbors, Eveline and Joe, who lived right next door to us, and Eveline always watched the house while I was running to school. If Eveline had to run an errand, I always did the same for her. I didn't have to do this trip to school every day as many days Jim didn't leave for work until I returned. Being a salesman, and being able to set his own hours, it was often possible for Jim to leave the house at 8:30. Most men in Montclair left for work at around 7:30 in the morning.

When we initially enrolled Jimmy in St. Cassian's School, they had an all-day program, and this was good for me, but shortly after starting school, they changed to a no lunch program, and this was very difficult for me to do. It meant driving to school in the morning and then driving back at noon for lunch and then back again for the afternoon session and then back again at 3 p.m. to pick Jimmy up. Because all this driving was not possible,

I got involved in the "car pool" which I never wanted to do. As a result of this, mothers were driving all around town picking up and dropping kids off. The only good thing about it, as far as I was concerned, is I got to meet a lot of lovely young mothers who had their children in the school.

Phillip joined Jimmy at St. Cassian's the following year, but Phillip had a different experience than Jimmy. Phillip hated St. Cassian's. I should have taken him out after the first grade, but I didn't and that was a mistake. To this day, he always talks about how much he hated that school. I think the difference in his experience as opposed to Jimmy's was that he didn't have a nice class. Many years later I spoke to women in Montclair who said that some classes were better than others, and for some reason, the children in Phillip's class were just not as nice as the children in Jimmy's class. When we analyzed it, we discovered that most of the children in Jimmy's class were the first children of large families, and the children in Phillip's class were the second children of these families. The women came to the conclusion that the first children were serious, responsible students, and, therefore, the teachers expected their brothers and sisters to be serious, responsible students, and they weren't. The high expectations of these teachers were not met by these children and, therefore, all sorts of problems arose.

St. Cassian's had an avant-garde method of teaching and grading. There were no grades. Everything was "satisfactory" or "unsatisfactory." Each child was supposed to advance at his own pace. This seemed like a good idea to me until Phillip, after having spent eight miserable years in this school, was about to graduate and the principal called Jim and me in for a conference. Jim was just recuperating from an eye operation and was literally blind at the time. The principal told us on the eve of graduation that Phillip had a 5th grade math level, and that she wanted to keep him back. We were shocked. We knew that Phillip could not spend another day at that school, and Jim told the principal, "Here is what I want you to do. You are to give Phillip his diploma; I don't care what the grade level is." He told her it was a little late to be telling us he was in a 5th level of math when every year his report card came back "Satisfactory." Of course, we should have known this, but the children never got homework, as this school didn't believe in homework, and since no one ever informed us of his lack of math skills, we just assumed he was progressing nicely.

The principal was really shocked by Jim's attitude, but Phillip did graduate the next day.

Before finishing up with the St. Cassian's school saga, I have to relate the story of the day that Jimmy and Phillip, who were about seven and eight years old, were coming home from school. It was a hot day, and for some reason they were walking barefoot while taking a short cut through a backyard. At the time there weren't many fences in town and the kids could walk through the yards between houses. They were carrying their shoes, and so, barefooted, they stepped on a hornet's nest. They were immediately stung by these bees all over their heads and feet, and any area that was exposed. They came running home, screaming with a few hornets still attacking them. I was in the house, and I could hear them screaming. Phillip, in particular, had bee stingers all over his ears. When they got in the house, I initially couldn't figure out what was wrong with them, and then I saw the stingers which I removed as fast as I could. When we all calmed down, I noticed that they were missing their new shoes. They told me they dropped them in the yard where they were stung. I was horrified. They needed the shoes to go to school the next day, and we really could not just leave these new shoes there. So, I said to Jimmy who understood that we didn't have the money to just go out and buy new shoes that we would have to return to the "scene of the crime" and get the shoes. He and I were both frightened of the hornets, but I put a slicker raincoat and hat and socks and sneakers on him, and we proceeded back to the house with the hornets. We drove the car down the driveway, and Jimmy jumped out, ran to the spot where the shoes were laying right next to the nest, snatched them up and jumped back into the car. It was a very courageous thing to do, and I was very proud of Jimmy that day.

While the children were going to St. Cassian's, Jim and I really got involved in school activities. We ran dances to raise money, and we entered a contingent of students in the Fourth of July parade for three years. The first time we entered as a parade participant, we had a marching group of boys and girls who just carried American flags. The second time was the Bicentennial Parade in 1976 and we had about 80 children in the parade. My mother made all the boys blue vests with gold ribbon on them and white jabots to make them look like colonial citizens. For the girls, my mother and I made colonial caps. The boys also wore tri-corner hats. Every child who was not away on vacation wanted to be part of the parade, and so we had a great contingent. All of my friends and their husbands took part in the parade. It took a lot of work to get this group in shape for marching, and our friend,

Gene Byrne, proceeded to have practice marches in the gym for a couple of nights before the parade.

My mother, Jim, Gene and I made a huge banner that was carried at the front of our group and it said, "For God and Country." Making the banner was a monumental job. First, my mother sewed all the fabric together, then Jim calculated how big the letters would be in order to make the banner stretch across the street, and I lettered the banner, and Gene and I colored it in. It took many days to do this, and the children got in on the action of coloring the banner.

As a result of the practices, the costumes, the banner and the enthusiasm of the crowd, St. Cassian's won first prize that day. When the parade was over, Gene Byrne had a big barbeque at his home where the bagpipers from the parade played patriotic music. It was an old fashioned Fourth of July.

The Fourth of July was always an important holiday in our house. Every July 4th, Jim would jump out of bed, run downstairs, put his John Philip Sousa marching music on the stereo and turn up the volume. The boys would be blown out of bed by the patriotic music, but they loved it. When they were little, they marched around the house with American flags. When they were teenagers, they didn't appreciate the rude awakening as much but we always had a great barbecue in our backyard and went to the fireworks.

Montclair 4th of July parade with Mark

It Only Happens Now and Then …

For the next couple of years, my life was centered on getting the boys educated and keeping them out of trouble.

When Phillip graduated from grammar school, we took Stephen and Mark out of St. Cassian's and put them in the Montclair public school system. Now all the boys were in the Montclair school system, and after the protective environment of St. Cassian's, this was a major adjustment for them. The interesting thing about it is they met all their long time friends in the Montclair public schools. It seems that when the boys were among lots of other children, they were able to pick out the people that they related to. All in all, it was a good experience.

Along about this time, Jim made a major decision that I think impacted our whole life. It seems that Phillip was falling into the pattern of calling on the phone and saying he was invited to various friends' houses to dinner, and asking permission to stay for dinner here and there. After a few days of this, Jim made a major announcement at the dinner table, and it was that everyone was to be home at dinner every night at 6:30 … no ifs, ands, or buts. If something special came up, and notice was given to us, we would decide if it was worthwhile to skip the dinner hour. Fortunately, the boys accepted this rule, and rarely ever missed dinner. I guess they were hungry. This simple rule allowed us to have some kind of control over four teen-age boys, and it worked. Another rule we had was that no one could come to the dining room table without a shirt on, meaning no t-shirts were allowed in the dining room. This seems like a crazy idea, but the boys were into it and always behaved in a civilized manner in the dining room.

On the subject of civilized manners, we tried to impart to the boys a sense of dressing properly for the occasion, for instance, proper dress for church, etc. On Christmas Eve, when the boys were in high school, we would all go to Midnight Mass. The boys had several friends who never went to church and were curious about our religion, having never been exposed to religion by their parents. We said their friends were welcome to come with us, but they had to be properly dressed … shirt, tie, jacket, etc. It was great to watch the boys arrive all dressed up. Some of these boys had never had a tie on, and Jim had to supply them with one when they got to our house. He taught a few of the boys how to tie the knot.

The boys loved going to Midnight Mass, and afterwards coming to our house for Christmas breakfast. Years later, one of the boys thanked Jim for showing him how a civilized man lived. This particular boy, Seamus Garland, married a girl, Patricia McGranahan, he met in our house, became a great husband and father, and is a wonderful Catholic today, and I think, would give a lot of credit to Jim for exposing him to a certain way of life.

Miscellaneous Montclair Memories

All of my energy and time went to raising the children. It was an awesome job, and one which I think most people are not prepared for. We go frivolously through our early life not thinking of the repercussions of taking on the responsibilities of family. When Jim and I had the four boys, all within the first six years of our marriage, we were so busy that our heads were spinning. A major portion of my time went to preparing food, doing laundry, cleaning the house, playing with the children and trying to have a life with Jim. Along the way, I met some great friends who helped me cope with all the responsibilities. The most helpful of these friends was a gal named Marge McGranahan. We met her through our church friends, Marie and Bob McKeown, and she was about fourteen years older than I and was a fountain of wisdom. She was a totally practical and fun woman. She was the best housekeeper I ever knew, and she imparted to me her knowledge of cleaning which was invaluable.

I was now in this big house, with no domestic help, and I was overwhelmed with the amount of cleaning that it required. Marge taught me how to do it efficiently and she showed me how important it was to properly shop and feed the family. I looked to her whenever I had a dilemma and she was always able to help me. In turn, Marge would always say that she got through some very tough times because I listened to her and I was able to see the humor in almost every situation.

Together we went through about 30 years of great friendship. She was my support system, when "support system" was not in fashion.

Marge was the mother of five daughters and one son, and they varied in age from eighteen down to a baby so she had vast experience with children of all ages. I remember when I would tell her about a problem with my children, she would say "small children, small problems; big children, big problems" and it was so true.

Marge was married to Cy, an absolute prince of a guy. He was the head of the I.R.S. office in Newark, a man of high integrity. We spent so many happy times with them at our house and at theirs. I remember one particular night, when we were having a big party at our house. We had a friend who was not above a little chicanery when it came to income taxes. After a few drinks, he was talking about his various nefarious schemes to elude the I.R.S. Our friend, Cy, who was partially deaf as a result of a World War II disability, would always shut off his hearing aid when this friend of ours was telling his tales. Jim and I always thought that was so funny. Eventually, our friend learned where Cy was employed and stopped talking about his schemes.

Marge and Cy were great dancers, and this led us to the chairmanship of various social functions in our church. These affairs took up a great deal of our time because whenever Jim and I got involved in something, we really got involved. My mother actually thought we were crazy to do these things, but we had energy and enthusiasm in abundance and we found such undertakings made life interesting. At least that was our philosophy.

Jim, Marge, Cy and I would spend hours, days and weeks on these affairs, but it showed because they were always a great success. Mostly we got involved in dances because that's what the four of us liked to do … dance.

We had great enthusiasm and that is the key to an interesting life. For instance, the four of us spent countless hours picking out the music for the orchestra to play. Jim knew all the great songs and he would write them down and give the list to any band we were thinking of hiring. If they were not familiar with the songs, we didn't hire them. We always believed that the right music made the party.

Marge and I spent hours on the decorations for these dances. For instance, one year we transformed our school gym into the Starlight Roof, which was a famous dancing spot in New York City. To do this, we spent hours in my basement, with our decorating group, dipping hundreds of wire hangers in a can of white paint and hanging them all over the basement to dry. When they were dry, we made black and white crepe paper flowers – hundreds of them – and hung them on the hangars. The day of the dance we suspended all of these on wires from the ceiling of the gym. The affect of this was quite startling and transformed the whole place. All of this took up hours of our time, but it was fun, and this is what we did while our children were in school. These affairs were major fundraisers for our school. Today mothers go out and work, but we worked at fundraising.

We actually ran three of these affairs for our school and all of them were rousing successes. I think that today I could have been an "event planner." I loved to do things like that.

All the while as I was preserving my sanity by "event planning," the children were busy doing what children do … mostly playing and boy scouting. They were all great kids and didn't give us a lot of trouble. We ran a tight ship in our house, but we were fair, and the boys were fair. The great thing about boys is that they are fair, and if you treat them with respect, they treat you with respect.

Every night at dinner, everyone got a chance to talk … except me. I think I was talking to the boys all afternoon, and making dinner so that when it came time to talk, I was really exhausted. Jim took over the conversation with the boys; and a lot of the conversation had to do with school, sports and politics. Did I mention that living in a house with all men is an interesting experience? We never discussed "girl" things. They were just not interested. In a house full of men, each man wants to be "king of the hill" including the father. Everyone wanted to be the number one person in the house. It is very difficult for the mother and wife in this situation. There are just not enough minutes in the day to listen to everyone who wants your undivided attention.

During the early 1970s, Jim and I went into the creative stitchery business. In the early seventies, most women were full time homemakers, and it was very popular to do needlepoint or embroidery as a hobby. Our business which we called Hamilton House came about in a strange way.

My son Stephen was sick in bed and I wanted to amuse him so I started drawing little soldiers. I was inspired by the design on the curtains in his room. I started drawing these pictures, and I discovered that I could draw anything as long as I made exact measurements of the picture. My mother had told me that to duplicate anything you have to find the center of the drawing and measure from there. I wanted to make the soldiers bigger so I would multiply everything on the design by four or by six and using this technique I was able to blow up the soldiers. I then decided to draw the soldier on a piece of fabric and then "color" the picture using thread instead of paint. The children loved to see the pictures coming to life. I framed the "thread pictures" and hung them in Stephen's room. Jim, my husband who was an independent salesman, decided to see if they would sell. And they did. The next thing we knew we were in the stitchery business. Jim could sell these like crazy, and we were up to our ears in stitchery. I had to draw the designs, and then bring the design to a silk screener, who printed them. The next step was to put the stitchery in a plastic bag with enough thread, instructions and a needle in order to complete the project. The stitcheries were designed so that a child could do them. For every order of a dozen stitcheries, we supplied a finished piece so that the store could display the project.

Completing the samples to include with the orders was an enormous job. Fortunately, my mother was a great help making the samples. As a matter of fact, every day after the children went to school, my mother and I would sit in the living room and stitch. We actually were so fast at this that we each completed a sample a day. In addition to this, I continued to do all the things a stay-at-home mom did. I actually think helping us with these stitcheries prolonged my mother's life. She actually came downstairs every morning prepared to work. Unfortunately, we were not in a position to pay her any wages, but she wouldn't have taken them anyway.

Our house was full of thread, fabric, boxes, and it was like living in a factory. Every Saturday, we cleaned it up and we never worked on Sunday.

Our son, Jim, and his best friend, Eddy, worked for us measuring the thread for the kits. We paid them ten cents a bag. Their job was to measure the amount of thread for each design and put them in a plastic bag.

My mother and I folded the designs, inserted a large needle (suitable for a child's hand) and instructions into the bag. We did this procedure for a while, and then the job got too big and we worked with a home for handicapped people, and they assembled the kits.

Jim could sell the kits with no problem, but the little stitchery stores were not able to sell them. Jim did get an order from Macy's which could have been the beginning of a great business, but at that time, it seems like many stay-at-home moms went back to work, and sitting around doing needlepoint and stitchery went out of fashion. The last big order we got was from a catalogue, and it was a big order. They sold out of our design, but they went bankrupt and didn't pay our invoice. They wanted to order more because they had outstanding orders, and I remember they paid in advance for the additional order, but they never paid for the original order. I think Jim and I decided then and there that we didn't want to live in such a tenuous manner and Jim and I cut our losses and Jim went in a different business direction. I actually was glad to be done with the business so I could get back to my life as a mom.

During our time as entrepreneurs, we had an interesting summer. That was the summer that my brother, Joseph, who was a career military officer, came to live with us between assignments. It was an amazing experience. Joseph and Edie had five children, same age as ours, and so we had nine children and five adults living in our house.

My mother at our home in Montclair with all her grandchildren but one in 1971: Stephen, JJ, Eileen, Jimmy, Mary Kay, Phillip, Cathy holding Carole Anne, PJ holding Brian, Rosemarie and Patsy (obscured) holding Mark. Tommy was born shortly thereafter.

It Only Happens Now and Then …

Amazing as it seems, we all got along ... I was in charge of the cooking which consisted of producing a dinner for fourteen people every day. Joseph and Edie were in charge of shopping for the food at the PX, and Jim got the easy job of leaving the house every morning to go to work and return at 5:30 for dinner.

Actually, Jim was a great help in keeping order in the house, or else it would have gone to rack and ruin. I am thinking about how we all fit in the house, and I recall that Joseph & Edie, Tom, who was very young, and Brian slept on the third floor, while Mary Kay, P.J. and Carol Ann slept in a Volkswagen bus (it had a pop up top and sleeping arrangements) in the backyard. My mother slept in the basement on a pull out couch. It was a wild time with all those people in the house.

My brother, "Uncle Joe," kept busy repairing things in the house which was a great help to us. All the children were busy going to activities which the town scheduled for children during the summer months. We had a regular routine. In the mornings, they went to arts and crafts classes, and in the afternoons, most of the time was spent in the town pool. All in all, it was a great experience for all the children. Dinner was always at 5:30 and after that, the children did some reading, and Jim took the girls, particularly P.J. for a walk around the town.

Somehow, I remember that Mary Kay and Grandma were in charge of doing the dishes, and there were plenty of these.

I believe they all stayed with us for at least four weeks.

One funny story that I remember from that hot summer shows how stretched our facilities really were. My sister-in-law Edie was a great laundress, and she was always sorting clothes before she washed them. One afternoon, I went to make a spaghetti dinner, and I couldn't find any of my large pots for the spaghetti and the sauce. Where could they be I wondered? I went down to the laundry area in the basement, and discovered the pots. They were all on the floor by the washing machine, and they were filled with socks, tee shirts, colored clothes, etc., soaking before being put in the washing machine. I couldn't believe my eyes … I believe that was the only time I really lost my "cool."

My mother was so great. At that time, she was living with us and helping out with all the work that was required to run our stitchery business and take care of a large family. My mother had a great sense of humor. I can remember the day that Joseph and his family left for his assignment in England. A limousine came to take them to the airport, and I thought my mother would be very sad to see him go so far away (Joseph was my mother's favorite child), but as soon as the limo pulled away, and we closed the screen door, my mother said, "Thank God, they're gone. Let's have a cup of tea." She was expressing my sentiments exactly.

While my brother was overseas, he left his Cadillac with us. We were to take care of it until he returned. It was a great car, and we drove around in it for four years. It was great for my mother's comfort. We made many trips to the country in that big old car.

Mentioning the "country" reminds me to say something about our summers with the boys in the country. Starting on the Memorial Day weekend every year, we went to our house in the country. This was a truly unique experience because this house had no plumbing, but it did have electricity. It had an outhouse and a well. The kids loved it. It was a liberating experience. Of course, if we had had a girl, I don't think it would have been good, but the boys were not into taking baths, etc., so the outhouse was not a problem.

Jim, for some strange reason, was able to adjust to the rustic life. My mother and I were able to make the house comfortable, cook meals, etc., but it was a big job. I wasn't wild about the country, but I did it for my mother because she truly loved being there. She actually would stay there by herself or with one of the boys for a good part of the summer, and we would go up on the weekends.

The area surrounding the house was made for exploring. The boys had great imaginations and they could play at all sorts of adventures there. A particular favorite game of theirs was based on the Last of the Mohicans. We had all faithfully watched this series on Masterpiece Theatre and the boys were enthralled by the story. When they got to the country, they would pretend to be Hawkeye and his Indian companions, Chingachgook and Uncas, and they would run through the woods. My mother had given us the money to buy them a souvenir of our trip to Fort William Henry on Lake George where we had gone on vacation. We spent the money on a "long carbine" for each of the boys. This was the rifle that Hawkeye carried. This was one of the best gifts the boys ever got. With their imaginations they became Hawkeye and Chingachgook and roamed the woods behind the house seeking adventure.

The boys were always running around in bare feet and shorts, and no one ever got Lyme disease although there were loads of deer up there. As I look back on it, I wonder how we avoided this problem because the deer would be at the back of the house in the morning eating apples from a tree that was outside the kitchen door.

The routine of the country was that we worked around the house in the morning, or we went to New Paltz to buy supplies, then we came home, unloaded the supplies, and went up to Lake Minnewaska to spend the afternoon. My mother stayed home most of the time with Mark when he was little because he was napping. I would bring some bread and meat and something to drink with me up to the lake and give the boys their lunch. It was in this lake that Stephen learned to swim. I would get in the water which was always freezing and he would jump off the dock and I would catch him. The water was very deep at the dock and although the water was very clear you could not see the bottom. Minnewaska seemed to us to be a bottomless lake where we were swimming and this added to the excitement. Plunging into the cold water was always a thrill.

Stephen loved the water and he was fearless and in a short time, he was able to swim. In the meantime, Jimmy and Phillip could already swim, having learned this skill in the Montclair pool, and they would be jumping off the rocks into this deep water. Phillip loves to recount jumping off the high rocks into the water below. I never really worried about them, as they seemed so confident. Years later, my daughters-in-law were shocked at the freedom I allowed the boys to have in this lake. I never did allow them to go to the lake alone, but I really wonder what I could have done to save them if anything happened. Thank God nothing bad ever happened.

I loved going to Minnewaska. It was so beautiful and peaceful. When we would get there at about 1:30 in the afternoon, there was hardly a soul there. Imagine having a great big blue lake with no one swimming in it except you. There were no life guards, or supervision of any type. It was a unique experience on weekdays because there were very few guests at the hotel on the lake.

I occupied myself by reading books. I would take a novel with me and read while the boys did "whatever." "Whatever" consisted of their swimming out to a cove and climbing up on the rock cliffs and jumping into the water. When they got tired of jumping into the water, they would go to the main house, an old hotel, where we were able to rent a canoe for a very nominal charge. The only requirement for the canoe was that you had to be able to swim. Every once-in-a-while, I would take a ride with them. This was great fun, and I used to talk to the boys about how I could imagine Indians long ago canoeing on this pristine lake.

Often the boys would take a canoe out into the center of the lake and jump into the water. I believe Mark was about six years old when he was jumping off this canoe and into the lake. I have to think that in some ways I was oblivious, but they all seemed like such good swimmers that I never really worried about them.

We would leave the lake at about 4:30, and the boys would be starving from swimming all afternoon. The great part of it was that when we got home, my mother would have a hearty dinner prepared for us, and we could smell it as soon as we got in the door. It was great. It would be stifling hot in Montclair, but evenings in the country got very cool, as we were in the Shawangunk Mountains, and my mother, being a real country woman, would make a fire in the stove in the dining room, and she would play cards with the boys. I never liked cards, and I would go to my room and read my book.

If we decided to stay there for a week or so, Jim would come up on the bus. I never stayed for more than a week because by that time, I had had it with rustic life. We would be running out of clothes, and I needed to wash my hair. Often I would leave one or two boys with my mother, but mostly it was Phillip and Stephen. Mark was too little to stay.

The most memorable thing that happened to me at Lake Minnewaska was the day I took the boys swimming to the lake and lost a most precious possession. I had changed into my bathing suit in an old locker room they had on the dock, and when I went to sit down to read my book, I noticed that the diamond was missing from my engagement ring. A sense of shock came over me, and I looked down into the skirt of the bathing suit expecting to find the diamond, but it wasn't there. I slowly looked down at my feet and all around where I was sitting, but there was no diamond. I called the boys. We all searched frantically, but it was gone. I was so sad.

I had to pick Jim up at the bus stop that night, and when I got there, I didn't know how I would tell Jim that I lost the diamond. The four boys and I went down to meet him. When he got off the bus, I said, "Something terrible has happened." He looked around and saw that all four boys were there, all in one piece, and seeing how upset I was, he said, "What could be so terrible? All the children are well." I will never forget how relieved I was. It was a great lesson in how unimportant material possessions are.

Everyone began to speak at once to tell him of how the disaster occurred. Jim reassured the children that it wasn't important in the big picture of life. After that experience, I never wanted to possess anything again that would cause me such stress. Years later Jim bought me another diamond to replace the original. It was a 25th anniversary present.

Although the house was pretty isolated, my mother and I were never afraid to stay by ourselves. My mother had no fear of staying there all by herself. She absolutely loved it, and often she stayed there with Stephen, and they wandered around the roads, and she told him stories about how life was like in Ireland when she was a girl. Stephen was truly her favorite grandchild.

One time the two of them spent six weeks of the summer together at the house. We would come up on weekends, and Stephen would tell us of all the great things he did with his grandmother. In the evenings after dinner, the two of them would walk down the road to a stream where they would wash up. Grandma would also wash a few items of clothes in the stream. She was like a frontier woman. I remember one weekend going to the house and Stephen had made a great set-up of soldiers all set for battle. Grandma had let him take over a whole room for his set-up. She really encouraged his love of history, and she bought him bags and bags of soldiers for his games.

I want to reiterate that once we were in the country house, we were really separated from everyone. There was no telephone or television in the house, and the radio reception was very poor because we were in the mountains. If anything of an emergency nature arose, there really was no way to get in touch with anyone. Fortunately, we never had an emergency at the house. I think God was watching over us and in particular four adventuresome young boys. As the boys got older, they often went on jaunts through the woods and would come back hours later and Grandma and I would have their dinner ready.

Grandma used to worry about them, but for some reason, I never worried about the boys. They seemed to be very strong, with lots of energy and enthusiasm, and life was a great adventure for them. I always admired that in the boys. As a result of all the time spent in the country, I think all the boys are outdoorsmen who love nature.

On many occasions, especially when autumn approached and the weather was cooler, the boys would be gone for hours. There was a path behind the house which lead to a cave, and the boys would go through this cave which was situated between two giant rock formations and come out on the other side on top of a granite cliff. The cave was very dark and once they entered it, they had to walk through a narrow opening and follow a narrow path toward an opening at the other end where they could see light. Once they had climbed out of the opening and onto the rocks, they could see for miles around. This would be the starting point for their hikes ... we used to call the hikes "death marches" because young Jim was in charge of them and once Jim started to hike, he never stopped. These hikes could be a little dangerous at this time of year because often the boys would see deer hunters, hidden in the trees, waiting to take a deer. In the fall, when the boys went into the woods, they always wore some red so that hunters could see that they were hikers and not deer. Actually the deer hunters were not happy to see the boys hiking, as it scared the deer and it made hunting them more difficult.

Phillip and I were discussing these hikes the other day, and he told me that they never ever got lost which as he looks back on it now was quite a feat because they usually traveled miles.

All the boys eventually became Eagle Scouts, and I think that was a result of all the time they spent in the woods. Mark and Phillip, as they became older, got into rock climbing. When Mark was about ten years old, he and Phillip would venture off into the mountains and would climb the cliffs. Of course, I didn't really know what they were doing, but I just figured that they were doing things that boys do ... having an adventure. As I look back on it, I am sure it was very dangerous.

The house itself was full of adventure. It had lots of small rooms and the boys were constantly exploring it. One small room at the back of the house was chock full of tools. There were double edged axes and saws and files. Once the boys took a large saw which was actually a two-man saw and they went into the woods on our property and cut down a tree. They dragged the tree out of the forest and back to the house where they hacked the branches off it and sawed it into firewood for Grandma's stove.

She was always sending them on journeys to gather firewood for the two wood burning stoves in the house. One of these stoves was in the dining room and one of them was in the kitchen. The kitchen had a very large stove with four propane gas burners and an oven and also a wood stove on the side with two spots for cooking. Grandma always kept this part of the stove going as it warmed up the house which was very damp. She would put both coal and logs in this stove. As I said she was a real mountain woman and knew how to do things that a city girl, like me, didn't know anything about. I actually learned how to make these fires and Jim did too. Of course, the boys could definitely make these fires because she was always teaching them. The stove in the dining room could heat the whole house because the hot air would rise to the bedrooms above. Because the house was really in the mountains, it got very cold there at morning and in the evening so the stove was almost always going. It was a full time job just to keep the fire going. Grandma always kept a kettle of water on the kitchen stove so that there was water to wash up in the morning.

This house had a deep well with a bucket which was used for bringing up the water. We had no pump; if you wanted water, you had to throw the bucket into the well and draw up the water. I always thought the water was delicious; it was so cold, but Grandma usually boiled the water and kept pitchers of it in the refrigerator for drinking.

We would leave the country house after Labor Day weekend, and we would make day trips in the fall because the foliage in the mountains was a sight to see in October, and we would return on Memorial Day weekend. A lot of things would happen to the house over the course of the winter. The area where it was located was a haven for hippies who would gather in the town of New Paltz. We were never surprised when we arrived at the house to find that someone had been in the house and had taken some old things such as furniture out of the house. The house was full of old furniture which came with the house when my father bought it. One of the things stolen which we loved was a Victrola which played old records. We used to wind it up and listen to records from the 1920s and 30s. It was great fun, and we were sad to discover that the Victrola was gone.

Another discovery we made one spring was a snake in the outhouse. Grandma would never go in the outhouse without first hitting it with a stick. When she did so this time, a large snake came slithering out. Needless to say, I got hysterical, but Grandma stayed calm as usual.

We usually started our annual summer vacation by first traveling to the country house for a few days and then leaving on our trip. One of the things about the country is that we always had to mow the lawn or the place would go wild. Either Grandma or Jim would do this, but as Grandma got older, Jim would do it.

One weekend just before we left for vacation, Jim mowed the lawn and then we left. We were going to one of our favorite places, Lake George. By the time we got there, Jim was deathly ill, the result of mowing a lawn that was two feet high. He had a raging fever, and it was a very serious experience. After that, we decided never to let the lawn get that high again.

After Grandma died, we continued to go to the house on summer weekends. I remember we went there the weekend before Jimmy went to West Point, and Jimmy and I took a long walk on the trails around Lake Minnewaska. During that weekend, the boys caught a snake and put him in our china closet. When Jimmy tried to get it out, the snake bit him so we were off to Ellenville to see if he needed treatment.

Because the house was near West Point, we frequently picked Jimmy up at West Point and went to the house for dinner and a weekend respite. Of all the boys, I think Jimmy liked the country the most.

It Only Happens Now and Then …

.

The College Years

Raising four sons is a mighty challenge, and I was determined to do it right ... if I could. I had read enough books and stories to know that it was very important for a mother to produce honorable men, and that is what I have tried to do. I think I have been successful at this. All of the boys are fine men. They may be a little difficult to handle at times, but that is really no longer my problem. They have very distinct ideas and very strong opinions. I sometimes think I was very tough on them, but I always felt it took a tough woman to make a tough man. I don't mean physically tough, but tough on principles.

As I drove them to various activities while they were in high school, and I had them alone in the car with me, I would take the opportunity to expound on my views about drugs, cursing, tattoos, immoral behavior, etc. Because they were in the car, they had to listen or pretend to listen. I think they got my message loud and clear. It was the best place to get their undivided attention especially if a boy was alone with me in the car. It was often difficult to get a chance to spend time one-on-one with each boy. Often when all the boys were in the house, each of them wanted to speak, and the result of this was that I was unable to concentrate on what was being said. In the car, I was able to listen to what was being said and respond. Sometimes, the response called for the "wisdom of Solomon."

The high school days passed quickly, and then we were up to college. Here was the challenge. All the boys were very close in age. They were all born within a five year period so three of them would be in college at the same time. Jim and I never really worried about how we would do this. We just knew we would do it, and with the help of God, we did. Of course, the fact that our first son, Jim, went to West Point was the linchpin for everyone else's going to college. Jim was accepted to Columbia College, but I believe the overall good of the family weighed heavily in his decision to attend West Point. Because he went to college tuition free, he gave the other three boys a chance to have more funds to go to college.

West Point was a very hard and stressful experience for Jim and for me. It was not easy for Jimmy, at age seventeen, to go there. The curriculum was not a problem, but the harshness of training was very difficult. I knew that, but Jimmy never complained. In the end, he got a marvelous education, gave back service to his country, attained the rank of U.S. Army Captain, and learned to play squash.

That sounds strange, "learned to play squash," but Jim loved being a collegiate athlete. He travelled to colleges up and down the east coast playing varsity squash. We went to all his home games and enjoyed watching him compete. It is interesting to note here that when Jim went to West Point, he had never played squash, but when he saw it played he thought he could do it. He learned to play in a short time, tried out for the team and made it as the last man on a forty man roster. It was a monumental feat. Not only did Jim learn to play, he ended up as the first man on the roster and the captain of the team in his final year. We were very proud of him and went to see as many of his matches as we could. To this day you can find his name on a bronze plaque in the gymnasium along with the other sports captains from the class of 1985.

While Jim was at West Point, we made many family outings there on the weekends. I would make a hot lunch on Sunday, and the whole family would jump in the car and drive up to bring Jim some great food and encouragement. Often we would picnic by the Hudson River. The boys were all good about going up to West Point on Sundays. It was a family outing. We would walk around the beautiful grounds. West Point is one of my favorite spots. As a matter of fact, if we ever had a visitor from Ireland, we always took them to see West Point. It is a spectacular place.

Unfortunately, due to security concerns, the campus is now mostly closed to outsiders. Visitors can still go on an official tour, but they are no longer free to roam around as they could back then.

While Jim was at West Point, we, Jim and I, wrote almost daily. Most of the time, Jim would send postcards telling us of the day's events, and I would write letters encouraging him to not be discouraged, as I knew how difficult it was. Jim persevered and in four years was graduated. We all went to the wonderful activities that surrounded the graduation. Our whole family was very proud of Jim's accomplishment, and we threw a great party (as a matter of fact two great parties) to celebrate the occasion. We all went to the graduation and then returned to Gordonhurst Avenue to celebrate. On the following Saturday, we celebrated all over again ... this time with our close friends.

When all the celebrating was over, Jim took Stephen with him on a trip across America, and they had a great time going all the way to the Pacific coast and back and many interesting places in between. It was a great adventure for them and gave them both a new perspective on America.

In the meantime, Phillip went to college the year after Jimmy went to West Point. Phillip had a checkered career in college, but in the end, he did fine. Unlike Jim, Phillip took an entirely unconventional path through college, but he did it his way, and we are happy that he later made good use of his education. When I look back on the adventures of Phillip, I have to laugh even though I sometimes wondered if he would ever make it to adulthood.

I remember once, when he was about sixteen, wondering what would happen to him, and deciding that I would "give Phillip to God" and let God take care of him. I ceased to worry about him. I had decided I would feed him and clothe him, but he was now in God's hands, and I had faith that God would protect him and He did, thank God.

I remember going to Phillip's graduation and Phillip introducing me to "his lawyer."

I said, "Your lawyer?" "What would you be doing with a lawyer?"

And the lawyer saying, "You didn't tell your parents, Phillip?"

"Tell us what?" I said.

"Well, Mom, I'm out on bail."

That's all I had to hear. I almost had a heart attack. Phillip had been arrested in a disorderly conduct incident in which he had been the designated driver. He had actually been working in the library most of the night, but afterward he met with a friend who hadn't worked and who after much drinking had provoked a police officer and got them both in trouble. It was a close call, but Phillip was fully acquitted in court and learned an important lesson. Long story short, Phillip did graduate with honors from Eureka College, the alma mater of Ronald Reagan, and we now had two college graduates in the family. He had earned the highest GPA of any English major in his class and was given an award by the faculty of the English department.

Next, came Stephen. Stephen graduated the day after Phillip, and the story of how we got to these two graduations is part of family folklore.

When it was coming near for the graduations of Phillip and Stephen, we wondered how close the dates of the ceremonies would be. We were shocked when it turned out that Phillip's was the day before Stephen's. There was great consternation in the family, as Stephen felt he had gone through college in four years and was graduating right on time. Phillip, on the other hand, took six years and, therefore, he was not "on time" and that was his fault and not Stephen's. Jim and I didn't know what to do, as we wanted to go to both of these great days. Finally, we decided to fly to Phillip's graduation, in Eureka, Illinois, by way of Chicago, and then leave immediately after the ceremony and fly back from Chicago to Newark on the last flight.

Jim rented a Pontiac Bonneville car for the trip from Chicago to Eureka. This car could do 110 miles an hour with no trouble. And we were going to need a car like this if we were to make the last plane from Chicago to Newark. Although I am normally hysterical when Jim drives fast, this time I knew that if I wanted to see Stephen graduate, I would just have to "close my eyes and pray." After the graduation ceremony, we said goodbye to Phillip, and Jim, Mark and I got in the car for the wild drive back to Chicago. Jim and Mark sat in the front seat and Jim told me to lie down in the back and cover my eyes. He drove the car, as fast as he thought was safe all the way to Chicago. Mark was looking out for police behind every billboard along the way. I can't believe I was a party to this, but it was very important that I get to Stephen's graduation.

We arrived in record time at O'Hare airport; Jim dropped off the rental car, and we all jumped on the shuttle bus to take us to the terminal. As we were the only passengers on the bus, Jim asked the driver how fast he could make it to the American Airlines terminal and gave him a generous tip. The bus took off in a shot and then we were at the terminal where we proceeded to run to the airplane. This was before the days of scanning luggage and people. When we breathlessly arrived at the gate, we were told the plane was delayed. We were exhausted, particularly Jim who had done all the driving. When we got on the plane and the three of us were sitting in our row, the attendant came along to ask us if we wanted to order drinks and Jim said he wanted three Jack Daniels. The attendant looked at Jim and looked at Mark and said, "Is he old enough to drink?"

Jim replied, "I don't know what he's having, but I am having three Jack Daniels."

And so, we flew to Newark where we had left our car.

It was about one in the morning, and Mark was now going to be the driver to Gettysburg. We arrived at Stephen's apartment in Gettysburg at about five in the morning, absolutely exhausted, and we lay on Stephen's bed in our clothes that we had worn all the previous day. We had to be at his ROTC commissioning ceremony at 8 a.m. so there was no time to change. And thus began a whirlwind day at Gettysburg. We were so happy to see

Stephen graduate with honors that it was worth the crazy trip. And now we had three sons out of college.

Next came Mark. After a somewhat checkered career in college, Mark graduated from the University of California at Santa Cruz with a degree in ancient history. Jim and I were thrilled to be taking a trip to California because we had never been to the west coast. And, of course, we were thrilled that Mark was graduating. Sometimes I wondered if he would ever do it, as he had so many things going on and he wasn't too focused on getting this education. He was a faithful fan of the Grateful Dead, and I wasn't too thrilled about that. He and his friends followed the Grateful Dead all over the country attending their concerts. But, thank God, they all survived. He ultimately landed in California and that was where he went to college.

The most vivid thing I remember about Mark's college experience was that he was in the major earthquake that occurred in 1989, and it was a truly frightening experience. Mark didn't talk much about it, but I remember waiting home in New Jersey for some word from Mark. He called us around three in the morning to let us know he had survived. We had not heard anything from him since the earthquake occurred, and since his college was right in the epicenter, we were not sure if he was dead or alive. It was a very traumatic experience for his father and me, but more so for Mark. He said he was in the library when it occurred, and he went underneath a library table to survive. Books and shelves were falling all around him, and it was a terrifying experience. I think after that, Mark gave up any thought of living permanently in California. Ultimately, Mark came back to New Jersey, and after working for several years as a stockbroker, he went to law school and became an attorney. I am very proud of Mark … I always wanted a son who was a lawyer.

Four Honorable Men

I went back to work when the boys started going to high school. We needed the money, as you can imagine. In this chapter I will tell you about my experiences when I ventured back into the workforce after we gave up the stitchery business.

One afternoon in October, when all the boys were in school, I was walking down the block and a gal I knew asked me if I would ever consider going to work. I said I might but I could only work four hours a day and it had to be flexible because I had to be available for any emergencies that might arise with my mother and the boys. That was not a problem so I went to work for a firm that sold some type of computers. It was the beginning of the computer age. I went to work one day and Lou Tischler, the boss, gave me a raise in pay at the end of the day. His office was in a shambles, and he needed me. He was totally flexible and whenever I had to leave, it was no problem. The interesting story here is that one day he was talking about how he needed a sales representative, and I told him I knew a sales representative … my husband. Of course, Jim had never sold computers, and I told Mr. Tischler that, but he said a good salesman could sell anything, and Jim was a great salesman, and Mr. Tischler hired him. Jim worked at this business for many years, and it was the income from this business that got our sons through college.

After Jim was doing well with Mr. Tischler, I left to take care of my sick mother and following her death, I stayed home for a while. I had enjoyed working and, eventually, I decided to venture out and find a part-time job as all the children were in school all day.

The next job I got was as a private secretary to an eccentric Scotsman, George B. Oliphant, who lived in Montclair and ran a very profitable "metals, minerals and ores" business out of the third floor of his house. He was a fascinating man in his early eighties. When I went for the interview, he and his wife both interviewed me. What he was looking for was a person of integrity, and I think he saw that in me. The person he hired had to be scrupulously honest, as he and his wife were often away for weeks at a time, and they had to have someone in their beautiful home that they could trust, and that was me.

It was a great experience working for George Oliphant. We worked about an hour a day; he made a bundle of money and the rest of the day we spent talking about his life and his adventures as a young man in the roaring twenties. While working for him, I learned all about the trucking business and how things were shipped around the U.S. I never knew anything about that, and I learned about the metals, minerals and ores business, and how this stuff was sold, and how a person could make a great living by being paid "a penny a pound." It seems Mr. Oliphant was an international broker and sold hundreds of thousands of pounds of this stuff all over the United States. He put the deals together and for his services he was paid "a penny a pound." I was fascinated that he was able to do these deals well into his 80s. All these deals were done on a handshake. He told me he only dealt with honorable men, and no paperwork was ever necessary except for the invoice we sent them for the commission. That was my job … to figure out the invoice … and it got quite complicated because we were dealing in English Sterling Pounds and French Francs. I really had to put my brain to work.

I came to regard Mr. Oliphant as a dear friend to me and my sons. He was a wise, wonderful, and witty man who enriched our lives. Jim and I felt that without his wise words on how to raise "honorable" young men, our sons would not have turned out to be the delightful people that they are.

When I first met Mr. Oliphant, I was just about to embark on the stage of my life where I would be raising four "teenage" sons, and he took a great personal interest in my boys. He had these marvelous old adages that he would share with me which were very appropriate to a situation that was going on in my family at that time. On the subject of "bad companions," he said, "If you lay down with dogs, you get fleas." On the subject of lying and cheating and the people who do it, he said, "Treat everyone as a gentleman until you find out otherwise, then forget him." On the subject of winning and losing, he said, "Win as if you are used to winning and lose as if it doesn't bother you."

How often I have used these expressions when dealing with problems in my house, and I always said, "To quote Mr. Oliphant ..." My sons now have all these quotes in their memories, and I am sure they will use them with their children when the occasion arises.

Meeting Mr. Oliphant truly enriched our lives. My sons were greatly influenced by him. It was his enthusiasm for squash that motivated my son, Jim, to try out for the West Point squash team. And Stephen related to Mr. Oliphant as the grandfather he never had. He loved to talk to him about the world of business, and he remembers fondly that Mr. Oliphant always encouraged him to be the best he could be. Mr. Oliphant kept telling Stephen that "there's always room at the top." Every year he invited the boys to his home for his annual Christmas party, and Mark, in particular, loved to go there. It was a whole new world for the boys, and George Oliphant couldn't have welcomed them more graciously. It was a great lesson for them.

When Jimmy got into West Point, it was as if he were Mr. Oliphant's grandson. He was so proud of this achievement.

Shortly after that, I decided to leave the workforce and go back to being a "stay-at-home" mom again.

I did that for a little while, and then one day, on a whim, I was driving around and I stopped at the personnel office in Montclair State College. I filled out an application for a no-brainer part-time typing job, and I was hired on the spot.

The next day, I was assigned to the office of the Vice President of Academic Affairs. I was sitting in the very back of the office doing some routine typing when Dr. Garrett, the Vice President of the college, was standing in front of my typewriter asking me if I was capable of producing a letter that he could sign. I looked up at him and said, "Are you asking me if I can type a letter that you could sign?" He said, "Yes." I said, "That's my business; that's what I do; I'm a professional secretary."

He said, "Take your things and sit at the desk right outside my office." And that's what I did.

It looked to me like I was now the secretary to the Vice President of the college, and I was. Dr. Garrett's secretary was out on one of her various sick days, and Dr. Garrett could no longer function with this type of secretary. He had to have someone who was there all the time. His secretary went out on disability, and now I was replacing her.

This came as quite a shock to all the civil servants in the college as I was not a civil servant, and there were civil servants waiting for this job. Be that as it may, I was now the Vice President's secretary. He was a very intelligent and super fussy man. Every letter and document had to be perfect; but I liked working for meticulous people. We got along fine, and being a secretary at this level was a "heady" experience. Wherever I went in the college, or whoever I called, everyone treated me with great respect. I was on a "power" trip, but I didn't abuse my power.

Part of the duties of this secretary was to direct students who were working in the office on a work-study program. As soon as I took over my position, I noticed that two girls came to the office every day at 1 p.m. on this work-study program, and they sat at their desks and talked for two hours. Finally, I couldn't put up with their lack of work ethic and I asked my boss who was in charge of these two girls, and he said, "You are." I asked, "Are you serious?" And he responded, "Absolutely!" That was all I had to hear. I immediately set about having them reorganize the whole office, under my direction, of course, and they were thrilled to do something.

When that was finished, I always had a job for them when they came to work, and years later, I met one of these girls in the supermarket. She came up to me and thanked me for teaching her how to work. It seems that when she graduated from Montclair State, she got a job in the college and was very successful.

I actually only stayed in this job for about two years, because since I was not a civil servant, I could never have a job of this stature without taking various tests and "working my way up." I was already "up" and was not interested in starting at the bottom. I left there with a great recommendation from the Vice President, and I returned, once more, to my role as "chief cook and bottle washer" in my home.

After being home for about one week, I was in the kitchen preparing dinner when the phone rang. There was a gentleman on the phone; he introduced himself as Charles DiLorenzo. He had a law firm in Montclair, and he had heard about me from his wife who was a professor at Montclair State.

He said that his partner, Arthur Krohn, had lost his longtime secretary and was finding it impossible to find someone he could work with. It turns out that he was even more meticulous than Dr. Garrett. I told Mr. DiLorenzo that I knew nothing about the law and didn't think my personality was suited to being a legal secretary. He prevailed upon me to just come and meet Mr. Krohn, and I did, never thinking that I would be suitable to the job. Mr. Krohn explained to me that they were going into the world of computers, and I was firmly convinced that he didn't want me. I didn't know a thing about computers. Finally, after much discussion, I took the job on a temporary basis. I said I would give it six weeks, and then we would see. As it turned out, a girl from IBM came to teach me how the computer worked, and I grasped it quite quickly. To me it was very logical, and once you "got it," you "got it."

In no time, I was able to produce documents such as wills and contracts with amazing speed. Mr. Krohn was amazed at how quickly I could produce a will on the computer when it took days to produce a will on a typewriter.

The only thing wrong with Mr. Krohn was that he was unbelievably precise and no errors were tolerated in any document. He told me perfection in letters, wills and contracts was his business, and there could be no errors. We would do letters over and over just to be sure they were perfect. I was having a little trouble with doing things over and over, and I was about to quit after four weeks, when Jim reminded me that I had said I would do the job for six weeks. I had given my word so I stayed the six weeks, and by that time, Mr. Krohn and I came to understand each other.

I thoroughly enjoyed working for Arthur Krohn. He understood that my family came first and never asked me to work late. He never wanted to interfere in my family life, as he knew how important it was to me.

He was a truly honorable man, as was George Oliphant, Lou Tischler and Dr. Garrett. They were all gentlemen, and treated me with great respect. Each of these men told me, in their own way, that they wondered what I would have been if I had been properly educated. That was an interesting statement, but I think that I was exactly what the Lord intended, a wife and a mother, and I was quite happy with that role.

It Only Happens Now and Then …

The Sneaker Debs Grown Up

I could write chapters on the Sneaker Debs, all of whom I am still in touch with and have been for sixty years since we first met in high school. The "girls" are all solid citizens. All but one of them married and moved out of Brooklyn. The one girl who never married and stayed in Brooklyn was my friend, Annette DeGaetano. Annette traveled to Germany when she got her degree from college and became a teacher in a U.S. military school. After traveling around Europe, and perfecting her French, she returned to the United States to live with her family in the Bensonhurst section of Brooklyn. She still lives there with her sister. Annette became a principal in the New York City Public school system which is no mean feat.

Betty Keane, whom I have known for 71 years, is like a member of our family. My children all refer to her as Aunt Betty. After an ill-fated marriage, Betty met a wonderful man, Tom Dawson, 43 years ago, and until his recent death he was a great friend of our family. We spent countless happy times at family weddings, St. Patrick's Day parties, and always New Year's Eve with the two of them.

Peg Casella Jeffers went to school with Betty and me. I have known Peg for 70 years. After graduating with a teaching degree from St. John's University, she married Tom Jeffers, a boy from the next parish to hers. They were married on the main altar in St. Patrick's Cathedral, had their wedding reception at the Tavern on the Green in Central Park, and flew off to live in Hawaii. All of this was very glamorous to the "Sneaker Debs." They have been married for 50 years and have two children and three grandchildren.

Anne White Sweeney, the first person I met when I was a freshman at Bishop McDonnell High School in Brooklyn, married Ned Sweeney, whom she met in an ice cream parlor in Brooklyn when she was eighteen, and Ned was seventeen. He always jokes that he married "an older woman." After Anne finished nurse's training and Ned became an engineer, they married. They have been married for 52 years and are the parents of four children and eight grandchildren.

Theresa Donahue Reynolds, the girl who sat in front of me all through high school, married Jack Reynolds who she met at a fraternity party at St. John's University where they both went to college. They married when Theresa finished college and they moved to Panama. Right after their honeymoon, Jack and Theresa traveled by freighter to Jack's new job. We all went to the pier to see them off. Theresa was the first Sneaker Deb to get married and when she left Brooklyn and moved so far away, we were very impressed. It was the beginning of a great adventure for them. They have been married for 53 years and had six children and thirteen grandchildren.

Marie McCarty Haddock was the madcap of the Sneaker Debs. After bouncing around Brooklyn for a short while after graduating from St. John's University, she traveled to Europe and also became a teacher for the U. S. Army. She married overseas and had three sons. After traveling around the world with her husband and children, she and her husband divorced and she found herself living in Texas. She became a successful attorney and continued to raise her sons. Then she met Gene Haddock, a cardiologist who had been raised in the Bronx, but had moved to Texas. She told me that he was the man she "should have married in the first place." They live on a large ranch in San Antonio, Texas, surrounded by their blended family. They come east every other year, and they never fail to invite all the Sneaker Debs and their husbands to lunch. They have been married for 25 years.

Marie Boyle Farrell graduated from St. John's University, became an 8th grade teacher in Bedford Stuyvesant (a real challenge) and went on to Hunter College to get a master's degree. We were very impressed with Marie's master's degree. She was one of a very few girls in Brooklyn to have a master's degree at that time. She met her husband, Jim Farrell, at a dance in Brooklyn. We all knew who he was, but we had never really met him until Marie started dating him. I guess the thing that everyone remembers about Marie and Jim was their wedding which took place the day after President Kennedy was assassinated. They were having their wedding reception at the Fort Hamilton Officers' Club in Brooklyn, but all festivities on the post were cancelled. Marie's father told them he had a contract and expected them to fulfill their obligations. They said they would hold the banquet, but there would be no music on the post because the whole country was in mourning. After the wedding reception, Marie's father invited all the guests to his home, and he then went to all his neighbors' houses and explained to them that his only daughter was getting married, and he intended to have music and dancing and so he did. It turned out to be a great affair. She and Jim have been married 46 years. They had four children and eight grandchildren.

And last but not least is Kathleen Gibbons Hoyle. I met Kathleen after I started working. She is a dear friend, and she and I are kindred spirits. Before we settled down and got married, we traveled through Europe together and had a great time. Although she has lived in North Carolina for years, we keep in touch via phone and e-mail. She has been married to George Hoyle for 46 years and they have five children and six grandchildren.

There is a common thread that runs through all these girls. We were all raised in Brooklyn with strong moral values, and we were educated by wonderful nuns who taught us about the important things in life, especially about God and family. We were taught to have respect for our elders, and ultimately, our husbands and our children. We were all smart and we made good choices when it came to marriage. We all married honorable men who respected us, and we respected them. I have been in the presence of all these couples on numerous occasions, and I have never heard a word of disrespect from any of them directed at their spouses. I think that the secret of a long and happy marriage is respect and communication.

Tom and Joe

I really cannot write this memoir without saying something about my two brothers, Tom and Joe, who have been with me all through my life.

I will start with Tom who is my older brother. For years in Brooklyn, Tom and I had the typical brother sister relationship. He didn't like girls, and I didn't like boys so I guess that was the basis of this relationship. I do remember that he was very protective of me and didn't allow anyone else in the neighborhood to bother me.

When Tom went to Brooklyn Prep, he became a different person, as I recall. Our relationship improved greatly.

What I remember most about Tom was that he was an altar boy at St. Ignatius Church, our parish. I asked him how did he become an altar boy, and he said, "Mom." When he was about six years old, my mother read an announcement in the church bulletin about "altar boys" and she immediately signed him up for the program. Being an altar boy was a big deal in Brooklyn. It required a lot of work … on the part of the mother. And these Irish mothers were committed to the task. Tom told me that Mom woke him up every morning at 5:30 a.m. so that he could serve the six o'clock Mass. He said he hated getting out of bed at 5:30, but there was no way to avoid it. In the cold winter mornings in our house, Tom would find his socks wrapped around the steam pole in the bathroom. This was the first place that the heat came up, and my mother wanted him to have warm socks on before venturing out in the cold. He said everyday he would carry his cassock and surplice to church. The cassock was a black garment, and the surplus was a white garment which had to be washed and starched, and that was something my mother took care of. She took great pride in having her son neatly turned out.

Often he would serve two Masses and after that he would go to the kitchen of the priest's house, the rectory, and he would be served breakfast. He recalls that the kitchen smelled delicious, and they were always cooking tons of bacon.

After that, he would return home, carrying his cassock and surplice, get his books and make the long trek to grammar school, which was about one mile away. No wonder he is such a hardy man.

Being an altar boy in the 1940s required a lot of preparation. One had to study all the prayers and responses in Latin so it required some brain power. In our parish we had about thirty altar boys. The boys trained long and hard for the Christmas services. Tom said that for the Christmas services there would be twenty young boys in the procession, six older boys would be acolytes, carrying brass candlesticks and lighted candles, two boys carrying incense and one boy, Tom's friend, Joe McLaughlin, was the Master for the Midnight Mass. His job was to direct all the boys as the Mass moved along. It was quite a sight to see these boys moving around the altar in perfect order in their red cassocks and white surplices. It was like a veritable militia of altar boys in a synchronized drill. Tom said it took days of practice to be ready for Midnight Mass. It was a great experience to go to Midnight Mass in our parish, and the church was packed with people who came from all around Brooklyn to partake in these services because they were so special.

Tom served on the altar all through grammar school and high school. Often, he would be called out of class while he was at Brooklyn Prep to serve at funeral Masses.

Tom told me that he did not pass the test to get into Brooklyn Prep (he was not a great test taker, for some reason), but my Dad, who was very active in our parish as an usher and a major fund raiser for the parish, and who knew all the Jesuits who ran the school which was located in our parish, took Tom and went over to see the headmaster. He somehow convinced him to give Tom a chance and take him into school. Needless to say, my mother and father were very pleased about this, and the pressure was on Tom to stay in this school, which he did. There was nothing wrong with Tom's brain; he just was not into taking tests. Getting into Brooklyn Prep, the best prep school in Brooklyn, Tom set the standard for the whole family.

I remember that Tom always worked when he was a boy. One of his jobs was to help the sexton, the caretaker of the church, clean and polish every Saturday. For his work, Tom was paid eight quarters. He said he thinks the sexton paid him in quarters because he took the money out of the collection basket.

Tom went to Fordham University, a Jesuit college located in the Bronx. My Dad paid the tuition, but Tom had a part-time job in the evenings to supply his spending money for books and social activities. He took the subway every morning and it took about an hour and a half to get there. It was a long journey, but I expect he did schoolwork on the ride.

When Tom finished college, he had a degree in physics. It was the time of the Korean War and because he was a physics major, he had a deferment which enabled him to finish college, but he was still classified 1-A. Being 1-A meant that he was going to be called up for service, and so when he graduated, no one would hire him. He then decided he better get the Army service over with and so he enlisted. He had a short career in the military because it was a two-year commitment, and he spent eight weeks in basic training and six months in Signal Corps School.

Then he traveled on a ten-day journey on a troop ship, the Maurice Rose, to Germany. He crossed the North Atlantic in November and he said it was a rough crossing. When he got to Germany, the Signal Corps equipment was different from the equipment he had trained on so he had to go to school all over again. The following summer he had a month's vacation, and so he took a trip to Ireland where he met up with me. I think it was Tom's idea that I meet him in Ireland, and I am eternally grateful for that. We had a great time together and we got along fine.

When Tom returned to the United States, he continued his courtship with Rosemary, a nurse at St. Vincent's Hospital, who he had met on a blind date. Tom told me an interesting story about their honeymoon. They were married on a stormy day in February and left on a trip to Canada. On the way there, they decided to spend the night in the country house. What a crazy idea that was. They drove the car down the unploughed road and got stuck outside the house. They were unable to move the car so they left it there in the middle of the road. They shoveled their way into the house, built a fire and went to bed. At 5:30 in the morning, they were practically blown out of bed by the horn of the snow plough which was trying to clear the road. Tom had to put his clothes on and go outside and move the car. I cannot imagine a worse start to a honeymoon, but Rosemary was a great sport and she rolled with the punches.

Tom and Rosemary spent most of their married life in Massachusetts where they raised their five children.

Tom always had time to help Jim and me whenever he could. He never came to our house without his bag of tools, and he could fix so many things in the house on one visit that he would keep us operating until his next trip. And if anything happened in the house, we would always call him and ask his opinion of what the problem could be. Just by telling him the problem, he was able to diagnose whether we needed a new appliance, whether it could be fixed or whether it was just something simple. I don't think we could have survived the first years in our new house without his advice. I consider Tom to be a truly honorable man who cares about all of us. He would be there in a minute if Joseph or I ever needed help. I admire him greatly.

Now I am going to write about "my little brother" Joseph who holds a very special place in my heart. He was my little friend all through childhood, and we got along famously. I guess that was because I was the older sister and somewhat in charge, as opposed to my relationship with Tom where he was the older sibling.

All of us agree that Joseph was my mother's favorite child. We decided it was because he was the baby in the family and that he had a great disposition and a full head of curly red hair. Joseph and I spent many, many hours together playing all sorts of imaginary games. We went to school together and to summer school together. I don't believe we ever had an argument; we were just great little friends.

As Joseph went through school, he proved to be a wonderful student with great intelligence. My Mom used to say he was getting that from the Careys (her family), but there was a lot of my Dad in Joseph. He was a charmer; he laughed easily, had loads of friends and he was a great dancer. When he was in the seventh grade, I taught him to dance, and by the time the eighth grade graduation dance came around, he was totally able to do the Lindy, popularly known as the jitterbug. Everyone loved to dance with him including my friends. If he was just a little older, one of the Sneaker Debs would have captured him.

Joseph, like Tom, was an altar boy, and so he had many of the same experiences as Tom, and that was a big part of his young life. I remember that when he went to college in Jersey City, every morning he got a ride from our house to St. Peter's College. The car arrived outside our house at 7:50 with about four other boys in it and off they went to Jersey City. I asked Joseph how he paid for the ride and he said Jim Rafferty, the owner of the car, charged each of the boys what they would pay if they took the subway and the tubes to the college. Joseph said it was a much better way to travel than the subway. I also remember that every morning Joseph would go to the store across the street and buy himself a buttered bagel with bologna. To this day, that is his favorite breakfast. In those days it cost twelve cents.

I remember that while Joseph was in college, and I was working, I gave him an allowance every week to keep him in spending money. I recall that it was only $2.00, but in those days, Joseph said you could buy a beer for ten cents. He said his "allowance" allowed him to socialize in the local establishments with his friends. As I think about it now, I guess that wasn't such a wholesome activity, but that's the way it was in Brooklyn. I remember that every night at 10 p.m., Joseph went out to buy the early edition of the Daily News and on his way back he would stop for a beer at the local establishment. Of course, my Mom and Dad knew this, but Joseph never abused the privilege and so my parents indulged him. As a matter of fact, Joseph told me that my father never came down harshly on him for anything.

The one trauma in our lives at that time was the day Joseph wrapped my father's new car around a pole on the Gowanus Parkway. He was coming home from a formal dance at St. Peter's when he had an accident. Fortunately, no one was seriously injured, but the car was badly damaged. This happened on a Friday night. In the morning, when my Dad looked out the window and the car was missing from its usual parking spot, he asked Joseph where the car was and Joseph told him "there was an incident" with the car. My Dad never said anything and they left the house and went to the subway to go to work. Usually, on Saturday, they drove the car. On the way to work, Joseph told my father the saga of the accident. He said my Dad took it very calmly.

My Dad called me in my office and asked me to go to the car repair shop with him. He didn't want to get my mother involved in it. It was too traumatic. To make a long story short, when we saw the car, we were amazed and thankful that Joseph had survived such an accident unscathed. The roof of the car was lifted four inches off the windshield, and the center post of the car was dented. But these guys, the repairmen, assured my father that they could make it look like new with no problem. We pondered what to do. Should we just consider it totaled or should we fix it? In the end, my Dad decided to fix it.

It was very expensive, but the interesting part of the story which I never knew until recently was that my brother, Tom, insisted on giving Joseph an unsolicited loan to pay my father back. That was a great generous gesture on Tom's part because at that time he was a young father of small children. Joseph told me that he paid the loan back with the money he earned for spending the summers of his college career in the Army Reserve Officers' Training program.

Joseph seemed always to love the Army, and when he was attending college, he joined the Pershing Rifles which was a trick drill team. He said it was like joining a fraternity. He loved all the pomp and circumstance of the drill team, and he was a "spit and polish" man. I can remember him sitting in the kitchen in Brooklyn shining the brass buttons on his uniform and spit shining his shoes. The Pershing Rifles competed in many competitions and won quite a few. My mother and I would go to these events when they were within traveling distance, and we were always very proud to watch Joseph participate. I think it was Joseph's love of the drill team that made him eventually make a career of the Army.

He told me that it was the only thing about which he and our Dad ever disagreed. Dad couldn't understand why anyone with a college education would go into the Army. I remember when I went to Joseph's retirement ceremony at Fort Monmouth, Joseph gave a speech and told everyone that his father didn't understand his choosing a military career, but he said listening to the military band play Garryowen and watching troops march always stirred him and made him happy and proud to be a Colonel in the United State Army. He was confident that he had chosen the right career, and the Army was very good to him and his family.

What else can I say about Joseph? He was always there when I needed him; he was a great uncle to my sons and he was a great brother-in-law to my husband. He is a man of great faith, and an example of how to lead an honorable life. I admire him immensely

It Only Happens Now and Then ...

Joe, me and Tom on Joe's 70th Birthday in 2008

It Only Happens Now and Then …

.

My Father, Joe Fitzgerald

In preparing my memoir, I gained a renewed appreciation for my father after noticing how he appears over and over in my story. Someone once asked me, "Where is this person now who had such an influence over your life?" She was referring to my father and the decisions that he helped me make at one time or another; for instance, the decision not to go to nursing school, the decision not to move out of his house before I got married, the decision to make the decision to get married. When she asked me that question, my father was already gone from my life, but he has never really left me. I think about him almost every day. He was a monumental influence in my life, as all good fathers are.

My father (far right) with his family and other farm workers at Knockhouse before he emigrated to the United States.

My father was always immaculately groomed. He had a beautiful head of black wavy hair until the day he died and he was very proud of it. He had his hair cut every week in the hotel barber shop. He always had his shoes beautifully shined. He wore a freshly laundered and starched shirt to work every day, and he was never without a freshly ironed handkerchief. (All of the above amenities were perks of working in the hotel business.) He always wore an impeccably pressed suit to work, even though he changed into his Superintendent of Service uniform when he got to the hotel. He didn't have to get dressed up to travel to Manhattan. He just did. That was the kind of man he was. I think he believed in setting a high standard for his family. To this day, when my girlfriends remember my father, they always say, "He was such a gentleman."

I never realized until I was thinking about my life for this memoir what an influence he had on the lives of others, and I will share a story to illustrate this point. When my father died, and was being waked in Brooklyn, we were overwhelmed by the number of people who came from Manhattan.

It was quite a journey from Manhattan to the Flatbush section of Brooklyn, and it was quite a tribute to my Dad and a reflection of the affection that these people had for him. During the course of the wake, I heard lots of great stories about him. For instance, I did not know that my Dad was placing young Irish immigrants with no skills in jobs all over the city. It seems that the word was around in the Irish circle that if you needed a job, "Go see Joe Fitzgerald at the Belvedere Hotel on 48th Street."

When these men arrived at the hotel, my dad was always very nice to them. He told them he was sure he could get them a job, but first, he had to teach them how to run the elevator. This was his way of giving them a "skill." So, he would have them come into the hotel on Saturday, a slow day, and teach them how to work the elevator. He said eight hours on the elevator was enough time for anyone to learn how to operate it. Once the person could operate the elevator, he would send him out to the various hotels where he had a network of contacts.

Many men at the wake told me the same story. They said that without my father's kindness to them, they would never have gotten started in the United States. These men were now successful at whatever they did, and they said it was all due to my father.

One man told us that he had been a laborer for years and could not do it any longer, and someone told him, "Go see Joe Fitzgerald." He said he walked into the lobby of the Belvedere Hotel in his overalls and met my father. He told my father his story, and that he could no longer do hard labor, but he needed a job as he had a large family. My Dad told him to go home, put some decent clothes on, come back on Saturday, and he would teach him how to run the elevator. Eventually, he got a job as an elevator operator in a great building on Fifth Avenue, and he went from there to being the doorman. A couple of years later, he came back to visit my Dad and told him how much he appreciated what he had done for him. He couldn't believe his good fortune. He couldn't believe that as a doorman, every time he got a cab for someone, they handed him a tip. He was making more money than he had ever made as a laborer and he absolutely loved his job even if he never got a tip. He told me that story at the wake. It was a great story.

My dad was a very kind and gentle man. I never heard him or his brother Chris swear or take the Lord's name in vain. He and Chris were great friends and never said a cross word to one another for all the years I knew them. They spent countless hours in each other's company because Chris and his family lived upstairs in our building. Often, my friend Betty and I would come home from shopping (we were always shopping), and my father and my uncle would be sitting in the living room. They loved to see us with our bundles and look at what we had bought. They laughed at our antics and thought we were fun. I remember the time I came home with my new mink jacket. Uncle Chris and my dad were incredulous to think that I had bought this frivolous thing, but they agreed that if I wanted to squander my money on these things, it was my business.

I don't believe my dad would have denied me anything if it was in his power to give it to me, and it was in my best interest. My brothers would tell you that I was "spoiled," but I think I was loved. I hope my Dad realized that I appreciated all his love and nurturing. He was a wonderful man.

My father was a devout Catholic. He was a member of the Holy Name Society and lived by its precept of never taking the Lord's name in vain. He was instrumental in bringing the Boy Scout troop to St. Ignatius Parish in Brooklyn. He was a faithful parishioner of this parish, and was an usher and fund raiser for his Church. He had great faith, and he was able to pass it on to us, thank God. That was his greatest gift to my brothers and me.

Thanks, Dad.

It Only Happens Now and Then ...

It only happens now and then
That there's a love that cannot end
And those who find it are but rare
This is the love that's ours to share

It doesn't matter where you've been
Or what you've done or what you've said
This love we know can never end
It only happens now and then

There'll come a time there'll come a day
This world around will fade away
Beyond that time beyond that day
This love of ours will always stay

It only happens now and then
That there's a love that cannot end
And those who find it are but rare
This is the love that's ours to share

My husband is an Irish poet. The above poem is my favorite poem of his. He wrote it one evening after we moved into our house where we have lived for some 42 years. He has a rare gift for writing poetry, and although his sons give him a hard time and don't always appreciate his poetry, they have to confess that he does have a wonderful talent. He has a great memory and can recite his poems when the occasion arises.

But a poet is never appreciated in his own time. I think that may be especially true in America, but when we made our trip to Ireland, and he reached Irish soil and interacted with Irish people, he was truly appreciated, and that was a great thing. Finally, he was appreciated as a poet.

I want to say now a few words about Jim to let him know that I always appreciated him. I knew long ago that he was a very special person, and I have lived with him for 48 years, and he has really never changed. He is always nice and kind … a true gentleman, as my mother had said long ago.

It goes without saying that I have had great contentment in my life as a wife and mother. This was all possible because I married the right man for me. Jim has been a great husband for all these years. He is a man of great integrity and kindness.

I will always remember how kind he was to the children in the evenings. At bedtime, Jim would bring the children upstairs, carrying the youngest on his back for a "bus ride," and settling them down with a story read from a book. Jim has a great voice and he made the readings come alive. The boys genuinely looked forward to reading time. One book in particular, *The Illustrated Treasury of Children's Literature*, was a favorite. It contained excerpts from great books and all the traditional nursery rhymes and poems for children. Jim also read the boys, a chapter at a time, novels such as *Treasure Island, Great Expectations* and *Huckleberry Finn*. Afterwards, he would quiz them on the readings. To this day he and the boys make allusions to the stories they read together and are good acquaintances with such characters as Long John Silver, Pip and Tom Sawyer. They even remember little details such as the fact that Captain Flint was the name of Long John Silver's pirate captain and his parrot. He started reading Huckleberry Finn using all Mark Twain's words exactly as written. He soon came to realize the use of what we now call the "N" word to describe Huck's friend Jim was not appropriate for the children, and so he changed it to "Aunt Polly's slave." This did not go unnoticed, however, as Phillip commented, "It's good that Huck stopped using that word."

Jim has had immeasurable patience with me and our sons, and always, after every trauma in raising four boys, he invariably says "that was a lesson in life … an expensive lesson," and it usually was, but he accepted all the responsibilities of raising four sons willingly. He spent countless hours talking to the boys and giving them the benefit of his life experiences. He never lost his cool, and when I lost my cool, he calmed me down and we moved on from whatever trauma was going on in the family. Jim is a faithful Catholic and he set an example for his sons to follow. He is another honorable man, and so are his sons, thank God.

All the things that Jim accomplished, he did with very limited vision, as he has sight in only one eye. No one would ever really know this, and our sons never saw him as handicapped, but he was. It is very difficult to have the courage to get married, and have four children and be their sole support with two eyes. It is unbelievable to do this with only one functioning eye. It never stopped Jim from reading to the children when they were little, driving them to track meets, driving them to college and all the things that great fathers do. And with all the interaction with the children, he showed them an amazing knowledge of the important and the trivial and a keen sense of humor … all qualities that our sons now have in abundance.

Now as Jim and I are in the sunset of our lives, he is taking great care of me as I cope with deteriorating eyesight. I am now more blind than he is, and we laugh at this turn of events. I wasn't supposed to go blind ... at least that wasn't our plan ... but God's plan is different, and we are coping with it. Jim has always been a loving, caring husband and he continues to be that way. As my mother would say, "He's a keeper."

At home with Jim in Montclair 1996

It Only Happens Now and Then ...

Some Happy Remembrances

I haven't said a lot about my sons in this memoir, but it's not because I don't appreciate how nice they have been to me and Jim. It's hard to write down the many things that happened to us as a result of these fellows. They brought us much joy just watching them grow and following their escapades through college and beyond. Those are tales for another book.

I do want to tell a couple of stories here about some things they did for Jim and me that we will never forget.

First of all was the Christmas that we got a little box from all the boys and their wives (Mark was not married at the time). In the box were tickets to Ireland and a two-week tour of Ireland. Jim and I were overwhelmed by this generous gift. It was such a happy Christmas. It was the first time we had our little granddaughters, Mary Patrice and Patty, for Christmas, and we were thrilled to have little girls in the house. They added such pleasure to the occasion.

The trip to Ireland was a great experience. A limo picked us up to take us to the airport, and it was a first-class tour of Ireland. Jim had never been to Ireland, and he loved it and to get such a generous gift left Jim and me speechless.

And then there was the Christmas that Stephen and Tara came to the house before Midnight Mass, and Stephen said, "Mom, I have a present for you." Since I was busy running around the house getting ready for the party we would have after Midnight Mass, I said, "Couldn't it wait until after Mass?" But he replied, "No. You have to open it right now."

So there it was ... a huge box with a big red ribbon on it. I honestly couldn't imagine what it was, and when I opened the box, it looked like a fur blanket. I really thought it was a fur blanket, and I remember thinking why can't this wait until after Mass? When I took it out of the box, I realized it was a full length mink coat. I was speechless. It fit me perfectly, and I loved it. Stephen knew that I had always wanted a mink coat, but I never really thought I would get one. Jim had told me if I wanted a mink coat, I should just go and buy it, but I didn't want to buy it. I wanted to get it as a surprise, in a big box, with a red ribbon. Stephen had heard me tell this story to Jim and he never forgot it, and he said when he made money, he was going to buy that coat for me. And this was it. That was fifteen years ago, and I wear that coat every winter, and I am never cold. I have gotten tons of compliments on the coat, and I always reply to everyone who comments on the coat that "my son Stephen gave it to me."

The next great surprise I got was a new car ... a gift from my four sons. Mark and I were driving home from my office in my junky car one day (I got all of Jim's hand-me-down cars), and we were going down a steep hill on a wintry night when the brakes failed. Mark was incensed that his mother was driving in this crummy car, and called his brother Jim to discuss the situation. The boys all got together and decided to buy me a new car as a surprise. What a surprise!

We were all going out to dinner, and Jim, my son, was taking the long way to the restaurant. Finally, he pulled into the Saturn dealer, and I asked him what we were doing there. Even their father didn't know about the surprise. When we got into the dealership, there was this beautiful gold car with all these balloons tied to it, and Jim said, "How do you like your new car, Mom?" I was thrilled and so thankful that my sons thought to get me this. They said it was a well deserved reward for being such a good mom. By the way, they ordered this car with a stick shift because they wanted me to keep my mind engaged for a long time to come … at least that's what they said. I love a stick shift car and I am still driving one today.

Mark, Phillip, Jimmy and Stephen

It Only Happens Now and Then …

The Best Gift of All

What was the most rewarding gift of all after a lifetime of living? It is the grandchildren. I am so glad to have lived to see "my children's children." What a pleasure and a blessing it has been to see my grandchildren bloom and grow under the direction of their parents. We have seventeen grandchildren and each one of them is a precious gift from God. We have seven grandsons and ten granddaughters.

They are all loved by their parents and it shows in their happy dispositions. Naturally, they are all bright and beautiful, and I should know, as I'm their grandmother. It has been a unique experience to watch my own children as they parent their children. They are kind and loving and constantly teaching their children about the important things in life. I would say that my sons have a grasp on what is important in life and they are passing their beliefs on to their children. Of course, they are not alone in the task of raising their children. They are aptly aided by the mothers of these children, who are also doing an outstanding job.

I am now going to end this my memoir. I started to write the memoir so that my children, grandchildren, nieces and nephews would know what it was like growing up in Brooklyn in the forties and fifties. I continued on through the present time – 2010 hitting some highlights and continuing some of the stories. It is really my memoir, and it's mostly about me and what I thought about as I traveled through seventy-five years of living.

What happened to my children as they went through life; that is, courtship, marriage, children, careers, etc. is material for their own memoirs. They have had very interesting lives, and they should tell the tales.

Epilogue

I am now seventy-five and Jim and I have just sold our house in Montclair. This is difficult for me. I am standing in the opening to my living room, in the house where I have lived for 42 years.

What do I see? I see all the people who were so important to me during the many years I lived in this house. I see my mother, on Christmas Eve, sitting by the fire, with her one drink of the year in her hand, watching as Jim and I turn the living room into a story-land place so that our children would be truly surprised on Christmas morning.

I see myself sitting in my favorite wing chair on a Saturday night listening to big band music while Jim dances around the room as he picks up the set-ups of blocks and soldiers that the boys had accumulated from a week's worth of hard play. He could make order out of chaos in time with the music. The room would always be neat and orderly on Sunday morning. What energy he had!

I see all my friends, on St. Patrick's Day, crowded into the living room for our annual party. I hear that lilting Irish music and the tinkling glasses and the witty conversation and the wonderful laughter that was going around the room. Around midnight, I can see the rugs being rolled up, and I can hear the Irish dance music, and the men and women getting up to dance Irish dances. Even people who had never seen Irish set dancing were dancing and loving it. Then as the evening wore on, I can see people eating my Aunt Peggy's Irish soda bread … ummm, so delicious. And when the party was over … about 3 a.m. … I see folks gathering for Irish coffee.

I see the years going by and then I see Christmas Eves again, and this time, the room is crowded with teenagers and young men who were friends of my sons. There were so many boys who had nothing to do on Christmas Eve. They went to Midnight Mass with us and then came back to the house for Christmas breakfast. They were all wearing, as we requested, a shirt, tie and jacket. It was such fun to see them arriving "all dressed up," and they were happy to do it. Jim and I always thought that everyone seemed so civilized when dressed nicely for this special occasion.

I see all their faces again, on a cold blustery evening in December, standing around the fireplace toasting my husband at his 50th birthday party, and they appear again and again at wedding rehearsal dinners and christenings and funeral repasts.

I see all my friends again, on a beautiful spring night, milling around the living room on the occasion of my son's graduation from West Point. And then once again at his wedding reception in that same living room some years later.

Now the room is empty. Friends have died or moved away; children have moved on. The memories are not gone, however; they are all here in this room and in my mind.

Appendix I: Apple Tart Recipe

In case anyone would like to carry on the tradition and make my mother's apple tart, here is the recipe. It is very simple.

This tart looks like a traditional apple pie, but my mother called it an "apple tart" because that is what it was called in her native Ireland. Also, the green apples have a tart taste and unlike a typical American apple pie, this tart only contains apples and sugar ... no spices.

To make the tart, you need: seven large green apples, peeled and sliced into about 1 inch pieces; 1 cup granulated sugar; and 1 Pillsbury pie pastry (comes pre-mixed and refrigerated) or your own pie crust ingredients. My mother used a packaged pie crust mix when I was young.

Prepare the top and bottom crusts as per the directions on the package or your own recipe. Line the pie plate with one crust. Pour the green apples into the pie crust, add the sugar, and cover with the other pie crust. Trim and make some steam holes with a fork.

Brush some light cream across the top of the pie and bake according to the directions on the pie crust package. Generally, you'll need to cook the pie for about 45 minutes in a pre-heated oven at 350 degrees Fahrenheit. If you stick a knife in the pie and it comes out clean, it's done.

Appendix II: Aunt Peggy's Soda Bread Recipe

My Aunt Peggy was famous for her soda bread recipe. She told me she learned how to make these round loaves in her hometown of Longford, Ireland. This is the recipe she gave me and I have used it to produce many delicious soda breads.

It is important to preheat the oven to 350 degrees Fahrenheit. Also, before mixing the dough, preheat a cast iron pan for five minutes. Then butter the bottom of the pan and flour it. Do this first because you need to be ready to bake as soon as the dough is prepared.

Dry Ingredients:
3 cups of sifted flour
1 cup raisins
4 teaspoons of fresh baking powder (1 tsp. for each cup of flour and 1 tsp. for the cup of raisins).
1 tablespoon of caraway seeds
1 teaspoon of salt
1/4 cup sugar

Mix the dry ingredients in a bowl with a large spoon and make a space in the center for the wet ingredients.

In a separate bowl, add 1 1/2 cups of buttermilk to 1 beaten egg. Then add 1 tablespoon of safflower oil to the egg and buttermilk, and mix together.

Gradually blend the liquid mixture into the dry mixture.

When the ingredients are thoroughly mixed (a spoon will do). Put a little flour on your hands, form the dough into a ball and place it in the center of the buttered and floured cast iron pan.

Brush some melted butter on top of the dough; make the Sign of the Cross with a knife and say a prayer for all who will eat the bread.

Bake the bread for 1 hour at 350 degrees. Test for doneness in 50 minutes by inserting a knife into the bread. If it comes out clean and dry, the bread is done.

Acknowledgements

There are many people who made a contribution to this book and deserve my thanks. My son, Jim served as editor, designer and publisher. Without Jim's efforts my "memoir" would probably have remained an unfinished work. My husband, Jim, and my brothers, Tom and Joe, contributed their recollections and helped me keep my facts straight. My nieces Mary Kay, P.J., Carole Anne, Rosemarie, Cathy, Patsy and Eileen, always encouraged me to write my stories down and complete the project. Their enthusiasm inspired me. My niece Anne Tracy read some of my first efforts and encouraged me to write more. My long time friends, both those mentioned in the book and those not, have always been a source of support and encouragement and are greatly appreciated. I want to specifically acknowledge dear friends Betty Keane, Marie Farrell, Kathleen Hoyle, Anne Sweeney, Theresa Reynolds, Peg Casella and Marie Haddock who lived my story with me, and my Montclair friends, Mary Anne Beattie, Kathy Carney, Marie McKeown, Nancy Miller and Anne Grady, who have been true friends for a long time now. I am truly grateful to all those who contributed to the "memoir" and who helped me attain this long held goal.

www.ingramcontent.com/pod-product-compliance
Lightning Source LLC
Chambersburg PA
CBHW030913090426
42737CB00007B/181